# THE OWNER'S DIVIDEND

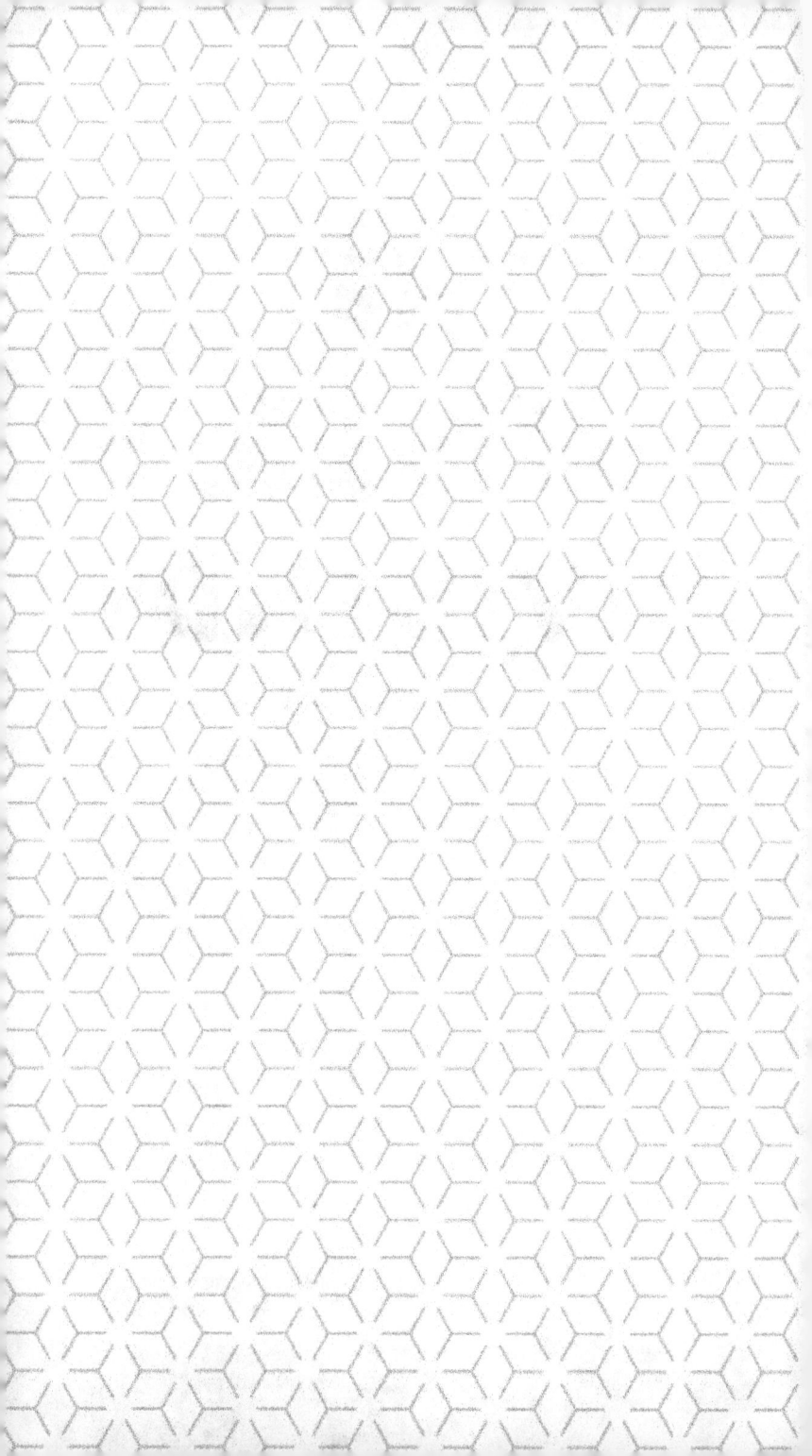

# THE OWNER'S DIVIDEND

## BUILD
## PERSONAL WEALTH
### THROUGH BUSINESS SUCCESS

# CAROLINE McINERNEY

Hartley
& Co.
PRESS

For Hartley, Will, and Margaret

# IMPORTANT LEGAL INFORMATION

This book is for general informational and educational purposes only and does not constitute financial, investment, legal, or tax advice. You should consult qualified professionals familiar with your specific circumstances before making financial decisions.

All stories, examples, and case studies in this book are fictional composites based on multiple experiences, with facts altered to protect confidentiality. No specific individual or company is represented. These examples are for illustration only and do not predict or guarantee any particular outcome.

The information presented is believed accurate as of the date of publication but may become outdated. Laws, regulations, and market conditions change frequently. The author has no obligation to update any information herein.

# CONTENTS

# INTRODUCTION

**M**ost successful business owners share a common experience: you've created something valuable, you manage significant cash flow, yet your personal wealth doesn't reflect your business success. If that sounds familiar, you're not alone—and you have far more control over this gap than you might think.

Growing up in a family manufacturing business, I thought I understood the full picture of business ownership. For us, that meant Saturdays weren't for soccer games—they were for working the outlet store at our parents' manufacturing plant. My siblings and I packed swatches, answered phones, cleaned the showroom floors. We optimized everything in that business—inventory turns, labor costs, vendor contracts. We had strong cash flow and solid margins.

But something was missing that I wouldn't understand until years later. During the hardest years, after a financial setback caused by a former partner, we moved from our home into a rental. We changed schools. Our parents were deep in the hustle, rebuilding everything. They worked incredibly hard to give us a good life, and they succeeded. But like many first-generation entrepreneurs, they were never taught how to build wealth beyond the business.

It wasn't until I started working with business owners on their personal finances that I discovered what the most financially successful owners do differently. They were capturing cash flow systematically, using tax strategies we'd never considered, maximizing retirement accounts we didn't know existed—all while growing their companies. The revelation was simple but profound: the gap between business success and personal wealth wasn't about working harder or earning more. It was about knowing the options available and systematically capturing value that was already there.

What I learned then—and carry now—is that hustle builds survival, but structure builds wealth.

-------------------------------------------------

## Hustle builds survival, but structure builds wealth.

-------------------------------------------------

# Every Owner's Advantage

Every business owner has access to what I call the Owner's Dividend—a collection of advantages that come with ownership itself. Not just the ability to pay yourself, but an entire set of opportunities most owners only partially capture:

- Financial dividends: The cash flow you could systematically transfer to build personal wealth, the tax strategies only available to owners, the retirement plan options with contribution limits that dwarf employee plans
- Strategic dividends: The ability to time income recognition, the power to choose between salary and distributions, the option to sell or hold based on strength rather than necessity
- Operational dividends: The improvements that naturally occur when you require consistent profitability, the systems that develop when the business must pay you

> regularly, the transferable value created by operations that work without your constant presence

- Personal dividends: The confidence that comes from wealth outside the business, the clarity in decision-making when you're not desperate, the relationships strengthened when financial stress lifts

These dividends exist for every owner. They're inherent in the structure of business ownership. You're not missing them because you lack capability—you built a successful business. You're missing them because no one showed you how to systematically collect what's already yours.

## The Uncollected Opportunities

In the chapters ahead, you'll understand why leaving these opportunities uncollected is costing you more than you realize. The S-Corp owner who coordinates entity structure with retirement planning captures thousands more in tax-advantaged wealth annually—same income, different approach. The manufacturer who started systematic transfers during slow seasons built more wealth than when he waited for perfect timing.

The agency owner's business became significantly more valuable after she required it to pay her consistently—not because she was preparing to sell, but because systematic operations create systematic value.

You'll recognize the five paradoxes that prevent owners from collecting their dividends, discover what happens when your CPA and advisor finally coordinate, and learn why collecting dividends during industry disruption works better than waiting for stability. Most importantly, you'll see that the discipline required to collect your Owner's Dividend transforms your business into exactly what creates transferable value.

# The Path Forward

This book is organized around a simple progression:

**Part I: The Wealth Gap** reveals which dividends you're leaving uncollected and why. You'll see how business strengths become wealth-building blind spots and why the conversations you're avoiding are expensive.

**Part II: The Planning-First Blueprint** shows you how to systematically capture your Owner's Dividend through coordination, timing, and structure. You'll understand why owners need fundamentally different strategies than employees and how to make your advisors work as a team.

**Part III: Implementation** walks you through collecting dividends during every business cycle—growth, crisis, stability, and transition. You'll see how this approach adapts to your reality rather than fighting it.

## The Complete Picture

When you systematically capture all four types of dividends—financial, strategic, operational, and personal—the impact extends beyond wealth. Business decisions improve when personal pressure lifts. Operations strengthen when they must support consistent distributions. Leadership changes when you're not managing from scarcity.

One logistics owner noticed the change when he turned down a large contract—not because he couldn't handle it, but because it didn't fit the company's direction. Two years earlier, cash flow pressure would have made that decision impossible.

## The Bottom Line

Right now, you're collecting some fraction of the advantages ownership provides—probably the most visible parts like occasional distributions or basic tax deductions. But the full set of advantages that come with ownership remains largely uncaptured.

Business success didn't happen by accident. Neither does wealth building. These advantages are already there, built into the structure of ownership itself. You've earned them by taking the risk and doing the work of building a business. They're yours to capture.

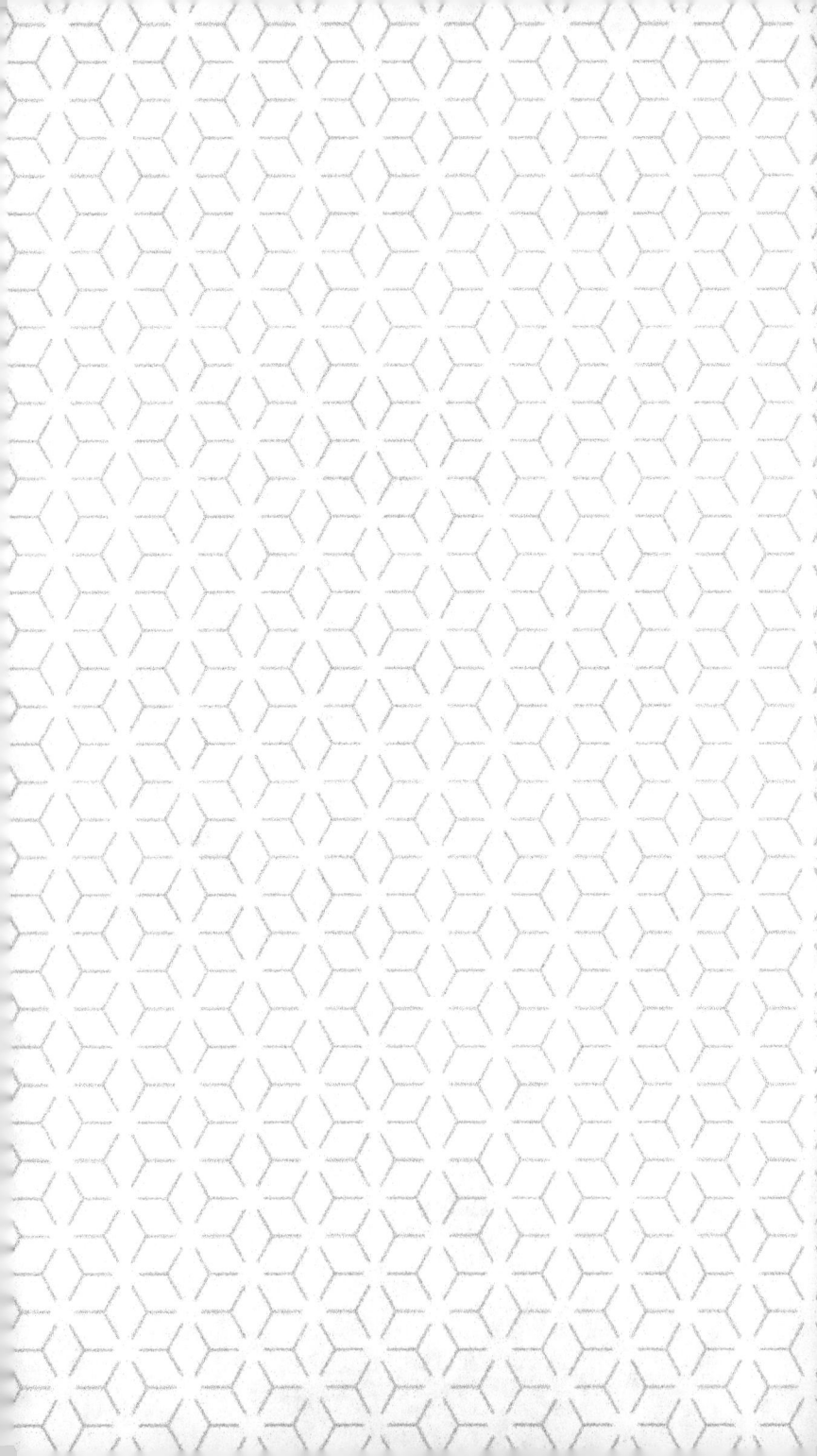

# PART I:
# THE WEALTH GAP

**Y**ou've built a profitable business that generates substantial cash flow, creates jobs, and serves customers. By every business metric, you're succeeding. Yet when you look at your personal financial statements—the success doesn't translate.

This disconnect exists because business success and personal wealth follow different rules. Your business conversations center on revenue, margins, and growth. The personal wealth conversations— what's enough, what comes after the business— rarely happen. Your business generates income reliably, but that income isn't systematically building wealth outside the company.

This section reveals why the gap exists. You'll see why treating your business as your retirement plan creates unnecessary risk, discover which critical conversations never happen in business families, and understand how entrepreneurial strengths can become wealth-building blind spots. The disconnect isn't permanent—but until you understand why it exists, you can't bridge it.

# CHAPTER 1

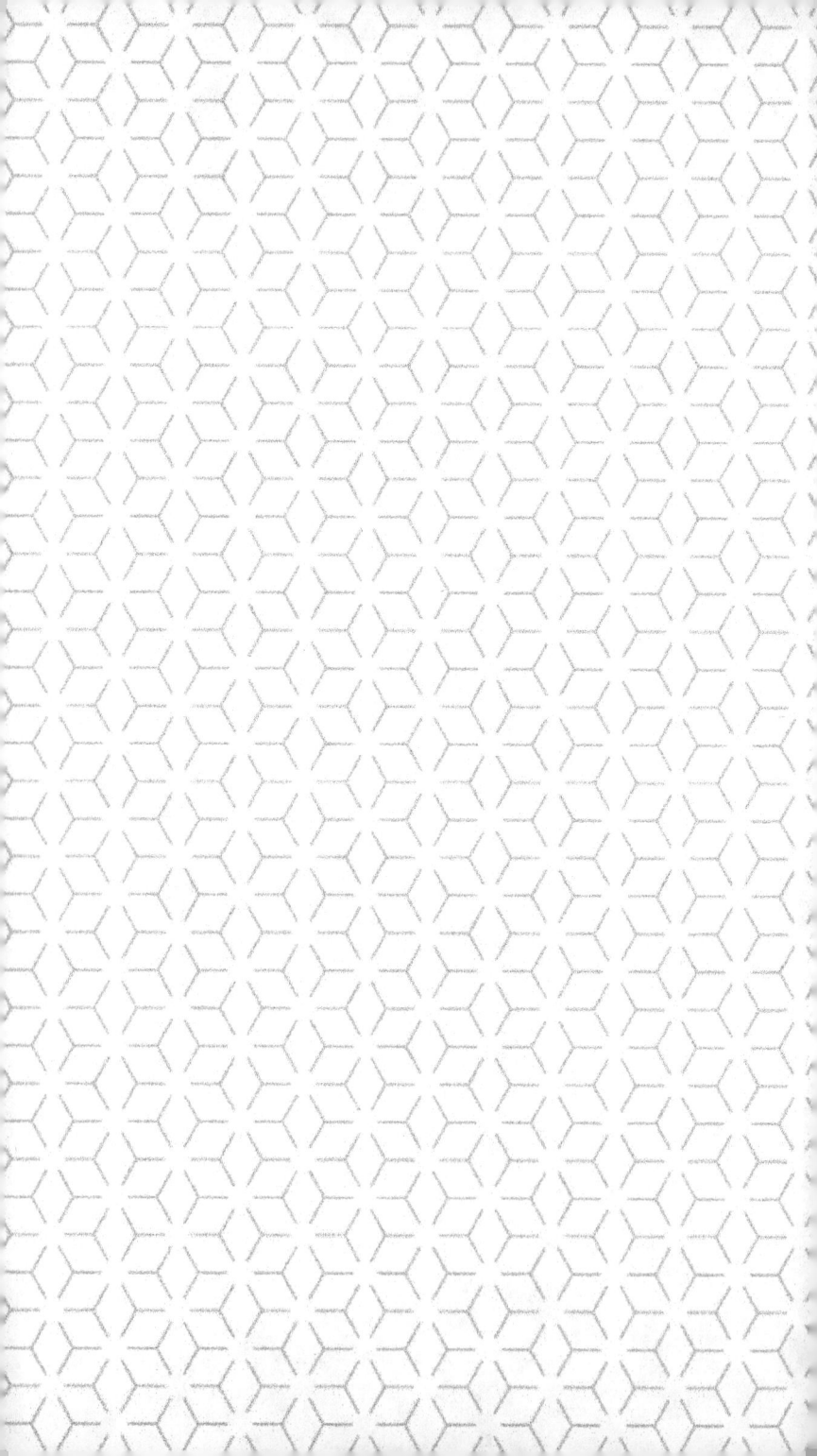

# WHEN SUCCESS DOESN'T SHOW UP ON PAPER

Successful business owners know every metric that matters—gross margins, cash cycles, customer acquisition costs. Yet ask them about personal wealth outside the business, and the confidence disappears. The numbers get fuzzy. The strategy gets vague. There's a reason this happens to even the most sophisticated operators.

Business owners who can intuitively read P&L statements and spot operational inefficiencies others miss often can't explain why their personal balance sheet lags behind. This isn't about financial literacy—owners understand money at significant scale. The gap comes from somewhere else entirely.

# The Invisible Wealth Transfer

---

**Every quarter, successful business owners make an unconscious trade—reinvesting profits into operations while personal wealth remains static.**

---

They create sophisticated financial controls for the company but operate without systematic personal financial strategy. They drive consistent growth in business operations but leave personal investments uncoordinated and reactive.

Meanwhile, taxes, inflation, and missed opportunities quietly erode what could have been building. A business owner with substantial income might pay tens of thousands extra in taxes annually simply because personal and business tax strategies aren't coordinated. Over a decade, that gap compounds into serious money that could have been building wealth instead of going to avoidable obligations.

The same strategic thinking that built your company can work against personal wealth when applied without understanding which game you're playing.

## Why Capable People Miss This

**Cash feels safe.** Business cash reserves enable rapid response to opportunities. But personal cash earning minimal returns isn't flexibility—it's opportunity cost. Significant personal cash sitting in checking loses purchasing power annually to inflation while missing potential growth.

**Concentration feels comfortable.** Reinvesting in the business built company value. But concentrating family financial security in one asset—even a successful one—creates unnecessary risk. When the vast majority of your net worth depends on one company in one industry, you're concentrated, not diversified.

**Attention goes to what's visible.** You'll analyze vendor costs for weeks to improve margins. But the 401(k) someone set up years ago? The investment accounts with high fees quietly draining value? Those sit untouched. No business would operate with that level of inattention to costs.

These aren't mistakes. They're business principles applied where different principles work better.

## The Real Cost of Delayed Planning

One logistics owner built a successful company over fifteen years, running seventy-three trucks across four states. The business had sophisticated financial controls—tracking fuel costs per mile for each route—yet personal wealth consisted of modest savings in a business account. No coordinated investment strategy. No tax optimization beyond what the CPA handled for the business. No integration between business success and personal wealth building.

"I keep meaning to address it, but the business always has more urgent priorities" was the common explanation.

Two years later, everything had changed. He had built substantial personal wealth—not by earning more, but by systematically investing cash flow that had been accumulating without purpose.

More importantly, business decisions began coming from a position of security rather than anxiety. When opportunities arose, evaluation became strategic rather than reactive. The difference wasn't just in account balances but in leadership confidence and decision-making clarity.

## How Wealth-Building Families Think

Most business owners think, "The business *is* my wealth plan."

Wealth-building families think, "The business *funds* my wealth plan."

They see business success as the engine, not the destination.

These families treat personal financial planning like a strategic business function, creating systematic approaches rather than reactive responses. They coordinate professional advice across tax, legal, and investment domains. They build personal wealth alongside business wealth, understanding these as complementary rather than competing objectives.

> ## They don't wait for liquidity events. They build during operations.

Strategic planning coordinates business decisions with personal wealth strategy. Professional coordination creates exponential value beyond individual optimizations. This isn't about choosing between business success and personal wealth; it's about creating integration that serves both objectives more effectively.

## The Choice Ahead

The company is built. The success is real. Now comes the choice: continue operating with the gap between business success and personal wealth, or bridge it through systematic action.

The next chapter reveals three conversations about personal wealth that most business owners never have—even in families where business finances dominate dinner table discussion.

## KEY TAKEAWAY

You can build a thriving company and still feel
financially vulnerable. The fix isn't working harder;
it's recognizing that business success and personal
wealth require different but coordinated strategies.

| Owner's Checklist | | |
| --- | --- | --- |
| **Metric to watch** | **Conversation to schedule** | **Action within 30 days** |
| Outside-business assets ÷ total net worth (baseline diversification snapshot) | With key stakeholders: share current numbers—what surprises you? | Draft a one-page personal balance sheet (assets & debts outside the company) |

# CHAPTER 2

# THE CONVERSATIONS WE NEVER HAD

I n our house, money wasn't hidden; it was everywhere. Invoices, payroll, trade-show costs, margin goals—the daily rhythm of a family business.

But somewhere in all that motion, an important element was left out: we never talked about the future—what my parents wanted beyond the business, what we were building toward as a family, how money could work beyond surviving another quarter.

------------------------------------

**You can talk about money all day long in your business and still never talk about personal wealth.**

------------------------------------

I didn't understand what we were missing until I started my career in financial services after college. At Putnam Investments, I learned about compound growth, retirement accounts, planning timelines—concepts missing from our dinner-table talk. Running retirement projections for clients, I saw what systematic planning could build— something my own family had never done.

We'd been running a business but not building wealth. We had income but no plan; ownership but no liquidity. The engine was running but nothing was accumulating outside it.

## The Three Missing Conversations

Over the years I've seen the same gaps in every industry and revenue band:

## "What is enough?"

Owners rarely stop to define what they're building toward, and this often creates tension between spouses. One partner wants the conversation; the other keeps deferring it.

But "enough" can't be defined in isolation. It requires honest assessment of actual lifestyle costs, including the business expenses that currently fund personal choices—the vacation planned around vendor visits, the company vehicle, the professional development conference in a desirable location.

Retirement expenses aren't just personal expenses; they're personal expenses without business tax benefits. That vendor-visit vacation might cost 40 percent more when it's not partially deductible.

And "enough" isn't just about maintaining lifestyle. Many owners plan for earnouts (staying on after a sale) while others want complete independence. Some are funding their own long-term care; others have different strategies.

The numbers vary dramatically based on these choices. But without the conversation, there are no numbers, just assumptions.

## "What comes after the business?"

Most owners treat the business like their retirement plan but never map what the transition looks like. Life after the business stays vague, unspoken. When a buyer finally appears, it's panic rather than planning.

## "What if I had to stop tomorrow?"

No one wants to imagine this scenario, but it's the test that reveals the truth. Could your family carry on? Would your finances hold up or unravel? It's the quiet worry behind every late-night anxiety that most advisors never address.

I saw this with my parents. After decades of building their company—rebuilding from a crisis, thriving again, sending kids to college, and eventually selling successfully—they had accumulated wealth but never went through the process of articulating what retirement would actually look like. They had the resources but not the road map. Without a framework for deciding where they wanted to live, what they wanted their days to look like, or how they wanted to connect with family, they spent years moving from place to place, searching for something they'd never defined. The hustle that built the business couldn't fill the gap left by conversations that never happened.

For owners, money without a clear vision isn't wealth—it's just resources that never become the life you worked so hard to afford.

---

## A business plan without a life plan is only half a strategy.

---

## What Happens without These Conversations

Without these conversations, you're operating blind. Every business decision carries personal financial pressure you can't even quantify. Should you take that risky contract? Expand into that new market? You can't evaluate clearly because business performance and personal security are tangled together.

In 2008, I watched this play out firsthand. The owners who had built personal wealth early could focus on business strategy during the crisis; the others were making decisions based on personal financial pressure. The difference wasn't intelligence or grit; it was preparation. One group had systems; the other had assumptions.

One business owner said it best: "I feel financially successful and financially vulnerable at the same time."

## The Compound Cost of Waiting

We never talked about how time affects these conversations. Like most business families, we assumed we'd have them later—when things settled down. But this is what waiting actually costs:

Every year you delay "what is enough?" is a year of compound growth lost. A forty-five-year-old who starts now needs half the monthly contribution of a fifty-year-old to reach the same goal. Every year you postpone "what comes after?" is a year closer to an unplanned exit. Every year you avoid "what if I had to stop?" is a year your family remains vulnerable.

Most business owners understand leverage—capital, talent, systems. But they overlook the most powerful form: time. Every successful owner faces the same logic: "My business might return 25 percent while the market returns 7 percent—why wouldn't I put every dollar into my highest-performing asset?"

That logic makes sense until you consider the risk. Concentrating wealth in one asset—even a profitable one—creates vulnerability that diversification can help manage. Your business success creates the urgency for early wealth building—not an excuse to delay it. Starting early means smaller contributions can grow into meaningful diversification over time. Early wealth building creates options that business equity alone cannot provide.

Time is working either for you or against you. There's no middle ground.

## The Starting Point

You can't fix what you haven't measured. Before any strategy, before any conversation, you need to know where you stand today.

A simple, one-page summary of what you own outside your business reveals the truth. Not revenue, not a valuation guess, but assets you could rely on tomorrow if the business disappeared.

This exercise often shocks owners who've been successful for decades. The gap between business success and personal financial security is real—but it's not permanent. Your business has proven it can generate income. The question is whether that income will systematically build wealth that works independently of your daily involvement.

Most owners assume the business itself is the wealth. But that assumption is exactly what creates the risk. The three conversations transform that assumption into intentional strategy.

### KEY TAKEAWAY

The three conversations business owners avoid—"What is enough?", "What comes after the business?", and "What if I had to stop tomorrow?"— aren't just uncomfortable, they're expensive. Every year you delay them makes catching up harder.

| Owner's Checklist | | |
|---|---|---|
| **Metric to watch** | **Conversation to schedule** | **Action within 30 days** |
| Personal-liquidity runway (cash ÷ annual household spend) | With CPA: walk through how much of today's lifestyle is funded by business perks vs. personal cash | Start tracking one month of actual personal vs. business expenses |

# CHAPTER 3

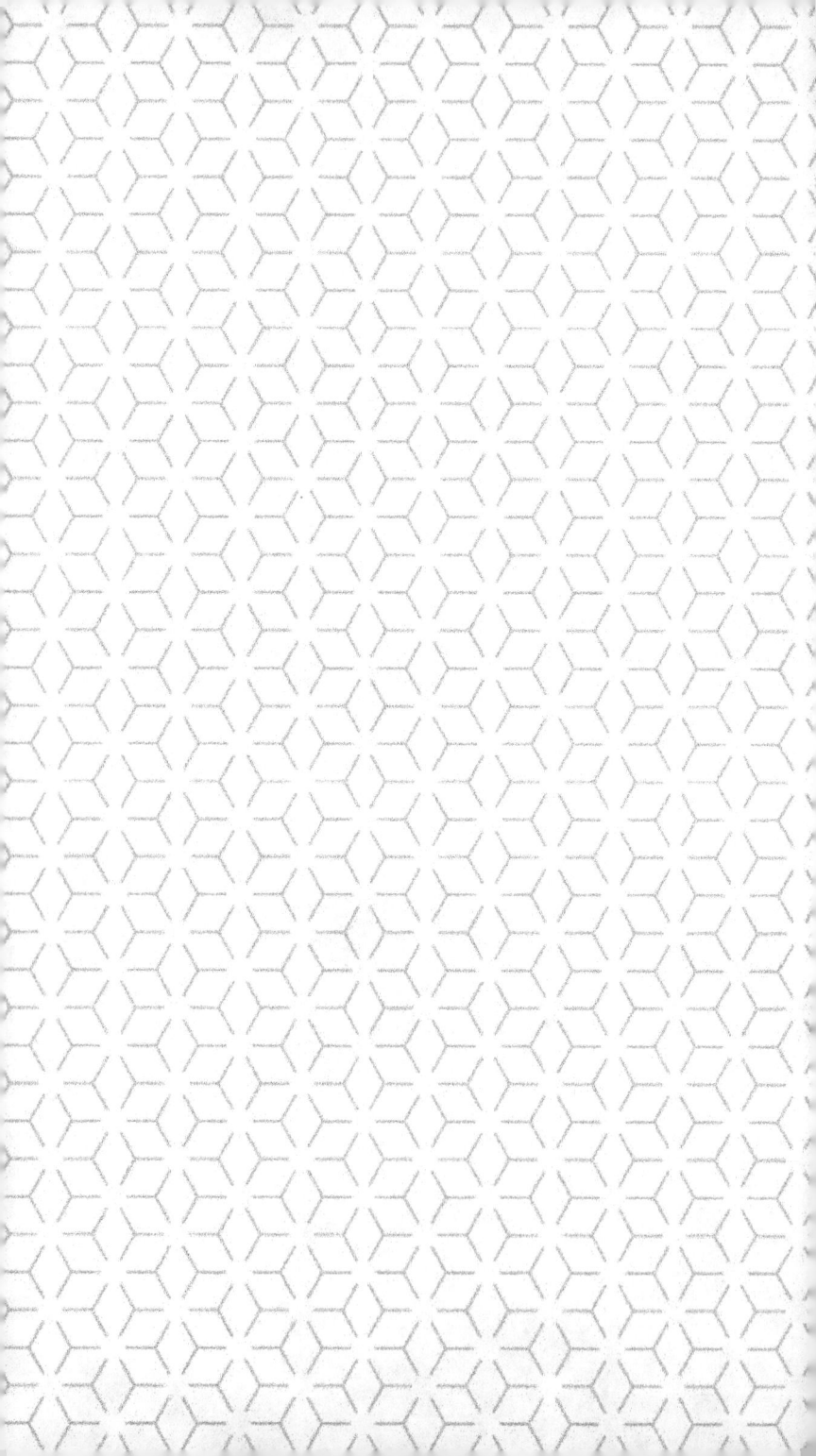

# YOUR BUSINESS BUILT INCOME, NOW BUILD WEALTH

**M**ost owners are making a single bet: that their business will fund everything—today's lifestyle, tomorrow's retirement, their family's security. It's a reasonable bet. It's also unnecessary. You can build substantial personal wealth while growing your business, and the discipline of doing so makes both stronger.

But this isn't what we're taught. We're told to reinvest everything, maximize business value, wait for the exit. Your CPA optimizes for this year's taxes. Your banker wants to see retained earnings. Everyone assumes the business itself is the wealth strategy.

There's another way.

# The Concentration Risk

When owners calculate their truly liquid wealth—what they could access in ninety days without selling the business or their home—the number typically shocks them. For most, it's a small fraction of their total net worth, often in the single digits to low teens.

Many business owners have the majority of their net worth tied up in their company—often well over half, with about a quarter holding 75 percent or more. This far exceeds the 10-20 percent single-stock concentration that advisors flag as risky. Meanwhile, with the median small firm having only twenty-seven days of cash buffer, you're part of what researchers call the "wealthy hand-to-mouth"—substantial net worth on paper, but little liquid wealth when you need it.

This concentration creates vulnerability that has nothing to do with your business performance. Your company could be thriving, profits growing, customers loyal—and you're still one disruption away from financial stress.

One owner was convinced she had a low risk tolerance. Twenty years from retirement, she said,

"I just want to be safe." But when mapping her complete picture—no debt, high income, fully funded 529s, solid reserves, plus 85 percent of her net worth concentrated in her company—the analysis revealed something important.

She was already taking significant risk through concentration in one asset. Meanwhile, her "safe" approach to retirement funds—keeping them in low-yield accounts over a twenty-year timeline—created inflation risk and opportunity cost that could impact her retirement goals.

Seeing the numbers brought relief and clarity. She wasn't conservative—she was concentrated. Understanding the difference changed everything.

When a single illiquid asset makes up the majority of your net worth—and for most owners, it's far more than half—diversification isn't optional. It's prudent risk management.

**The discipline that builds personal wealth is the same discipline that builds business value.**

## The Quarterly Challenge

A commercial flooring company owner with twelve installation crews and $8 million in annual revenue had been reinvesting every extra dollar back into inventory and new hires for years. The business was growing, but personal net worth barely moved.

Cash kept building up in the business, but the fear was always the same—what if it was needed for payroll? What if there was a slow quarter?

With professional guidance, the owner decided to try something modest: systematic quarterly transfers of 5 percent of net profit to personal wealth building. Not enough to hurt the business, but enough to matter over time.

The first quarter was chaos. To pay that consistent amount required cleaner books than existed. Cash flow was unpredictable not because of sales, but because of sloppy operations. Everything had to be cleaned up just to know what 5 percent actually meant.

By the second quarter, something shifted. To ensure the transfer could be made, the owner built buffer systems. Collections tightened. Forecasting became more careful. Business expenses were separated from personal ones that had crept in over the years.

## Unexpected Value

The systematic transfers were doing more than building personal wealth—they were making the business more valuable.

To pay consistently required building predictable cash flow, cleaning up books, and creating operations that worked without constant involvement. Within eighteen months, over $130,000 in personal wealth had built outside the business. But more surprisingly, when the business was valued, it had increased significantly since starting the systematic transfers.

The goal wasn't to build sellable value—just to create consistent owner pay. But that's exactly what happened. A business that can pay its owner consistently is a business someone else would want to buy. Buyers pay premiums for predictable profits and owner independence.

The systematic transfers forced exactly what creates transferable value: predictable cash flow, clean operations, systems that work without constant oversight. The fear that holds most owners back—that transfers weaken the business—is backward.

The discipline that builds personal wealth is the same discipline that builds business value.

## The Resistance

Yet every entrepreneurial instinct resists this separation.

> "That money could generate 25 percent returns if I reinvested it in the business."

> "I'm taking capital away from my highest-performing asset."

> "This feels like I'm betting against my own success."

These concerns make sense—your business probably is your highest-performing asset. But that's exactly the problem. When your income, your wealth, and your family's security all depend on one asset—even an excellent one—you're not diversified; you're concentrated. And concentration, no matter how profitable, creates vulnerability.

The businesses that create the most personal wealth for their owners share one characteristic: they don't require the owner's daily involvement to generate income. If your business can't run without you for more than a few weeks, you don't have an income-generating asset—you have a high-paying job with equity.

## Two Paths

Another owner runs a $3 million consulting firm with great margins and steady clients. The biggest client, generating 40 percent of revenue, has been there for eight years. The owner pays herself $200,000 annually and reinvests everything else.

She's been waiting for the perfect exit for five years. Her CPA says she's doing everything right— maximizing retained earnings, minimizing current taxes. Net worth is 90 percent concentrated in the business.

The flooring company owner started in the same position. The difference? One stopped waiting and started building. Not instead of growing the business, but alongside it. The discipline of systematic transfers didn't just build personal wealth—it built a better business.

The bet that your business will take care of everything is reasonable. It's also unnecessary. You can build substantial personal wealth while growing your business. The only question is whether you'll start now or keep waiting for perfect conditions that rarely align.

Your business has proven it can generate income. Now it's time for that income to build wealth that doesn't depend on next quarter's results.

## KEY TAKEAWAY

Your business is the income engine, not the retirement plan. When the majority of wealth sits in the company, you're holding a single—however excellent—bet. The discipline of paying yourself systematically doesn't weaken your business; it forces exactly the improvements that create transferable value.

| Owner's Checklist | | |
|---|---|---|
| **Metric to watch** | **Conversation to schedule** | **Action within 30 days** |
| Business-equity concentration % (company value ÷ net worth) | CPA + advisor: map sale value vs. salary/dividend mix & tax impact | Set automatic quarterly transfer from business to personal account (work with CPA/advisor on amount*) |

*Note: The systems you build to sustain these transfers will strengthen your business, not weaken it.*

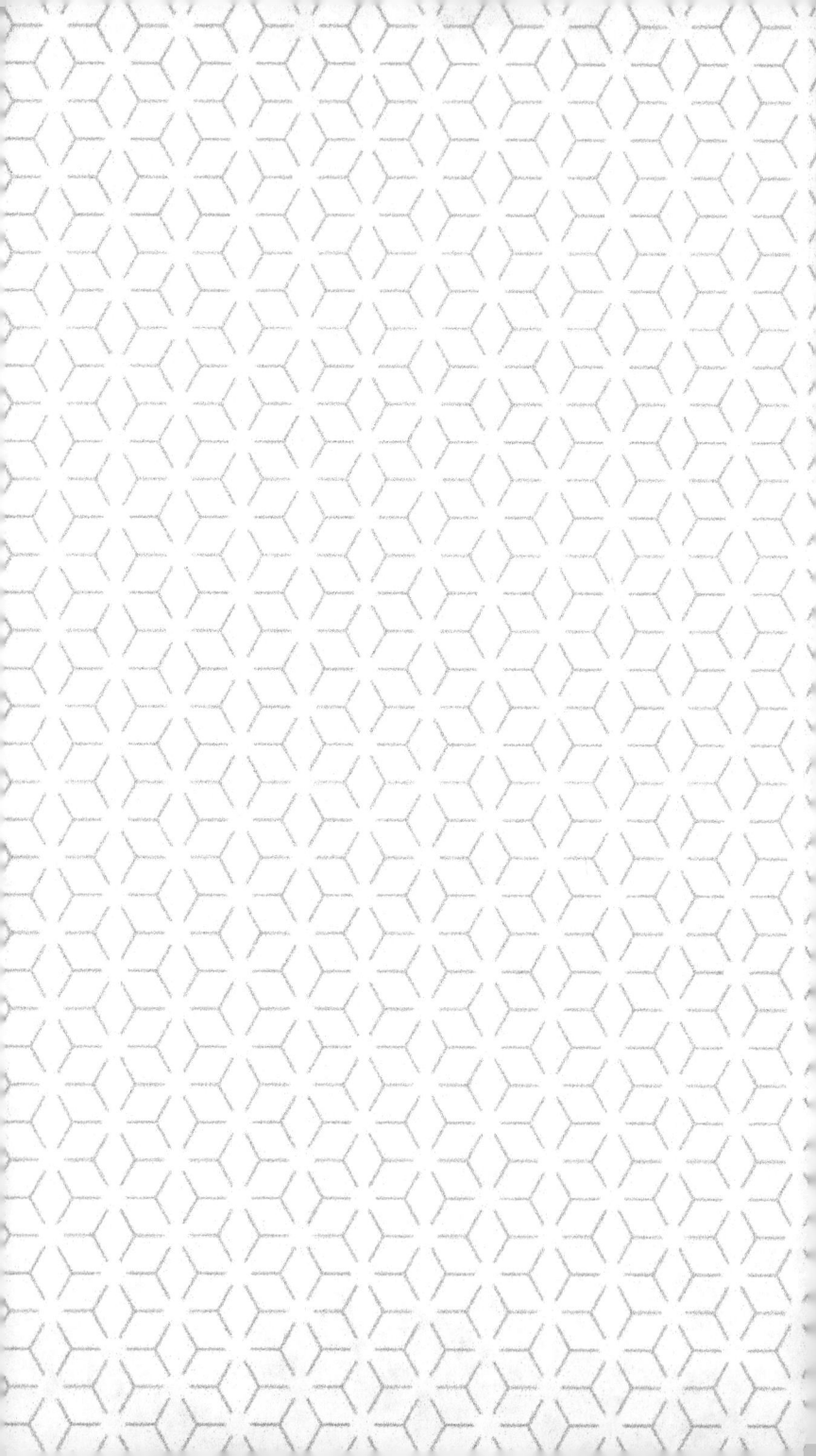

# CHAPTER 4

# THE ENTREPRENEUR'S PARADOX

According to Federal Reserve data, the median self-employed household's net worth is roughly four times that of employee households. Yet multiple surveys find fewer than half of owners say they're on track for retirement, and about a third report no retirement savings plan. Strong business results don't automatically translate into confident personal wealth management.

# The Entrepreneur's Paradox

--------------------------------------------------

**The Entrepreneur's Paradox: the very traits that drive business success can undermine personal wealth building.**

--------------------------------------------------

In the previous chapter, you saw how disciplined transfers created unexpected value for the commercial flooring owner. But if the solution is that simple, why don't more owners do it?

I've seen this pattern dozens of times: brilliant owners who know their numbers cold—gross margins, customer concentration, cash conversion cycles—but can't explain why they have so little personal wealth to show for their success.

They're experiencing what I call the Entrepreneur's Paradox: the very traits that drive business success can undermine personal wealth building. The frameworks that built your company need different application for wealth building. The exact mental models and behavioral patterns that make you successful in business can undercut personal wealth.

Entrepreneurial success creates specific blind spots that make the obvious feel impossible. This paradox shows up in five distinct ways.

# The Five Patterns

## Paradox #1: The Liquidity Trap

**Business Strength:** Substantial cash reserves for opportunities and emergencies. Cash is optionality and power.

**Wealth Blind Spot:** Holding too much personal cash earning 0.5 percent instead of investing for long-term growth. That "safety" becomes the biggest threat to your financial future.

Leave $100,000 in a savings account at 0.5 percent APY for twenty years and it becomes ~$110,500. Invest it in a diversified portfolio at 7 percent annually, and it could become ~$387,000. That "safe" decision costs you $276,500 in potential growth.

It's natural to apply the same liquidity thinking to both business and personal wealth, but your retirement is twenty years away—not twenty days.

## Paradox #2: The Control Obsession

**Business Strength:** You built your company through direct influence—every lever pulled, every result earned.

**Wealth Blind Spot:** You avoid investing because you can't control daily outcomes. Or you overmanage your portfolio, treating it like an extension of your business.

This shows up in two patterns: picking stocks because you "know the industry" or avoiding investing because "you can't control the market." Both approaches fail because long-term investing works best when you don't interfere. Delegation feels like risk. But in investing, discipline and process outperform action.

## Paradox #3: The Reinvestment Compulsion

**Business Strength:** Reinvesting profits for growth works. Your business generates returns better than any outside investment.

**Wealth Blind Spot:** You never build wealth outside the business. Every dollar goes back in. You justify it logically, but you've created hidden fragility.

This paradox becomes particularly challenging over time because it compounds. What happens if your industry gets disrupted or a recession cuts your revenue in half? You've put your family's future on one bet; even a great bet is still a single bet. Reinvestment becomes a habit reinforced by success, but it ignores external risk and dependency.

The pattern intensifies during industry transformations. Every generation of owners faces their version: AI and automation today, the internet in the '90s, computerization in the '80s. When competitors adopt capabilities you don't have yet or regulations reshape your market overnight, the pressure to put every dollar back into the business multiplies. You tell yourself you'll diversify "after this upgrade," but the upgrades never end—they just shift to different challenges. The owners who thrive build wealth especially during change, not after it.

You've probably heard "your business is your best investment." That's true—right up until it isn't. Industry data suggests many companies that go to market don't sell—some estimates put successful sales at only 20-30%. Even the best investment needs diversification.

## Paradox #4: The Optimization Gap

**Business Strength:** You optimize everything. You chase 2 percent cost savings like it's your job—because it is.

**Wealth Blind Spot:** You overlook inefficiencies in your personal finances: high investment fees, outdated insurance, mediocre performance are left untouched.

I've watched owners debate a $75,000 equipment purchase for months yet never review a $400,000 IRA. If you're paying 1 percent for advice, using higher-cost active funds (~0.7 percent), plus the typical investor "behavior gap" (~1 percent), that's roughly 2.5 percent in annual drag. On

$400,000, that's $10,000 in year one alone. Over two decades, that compounds to hundreds of thousands in foregone wealth.

Personal finance feels passive and less urgent than operations. But the drag is real, and the numbers are big.

## Paradox #5: The Timeline Confusion

**Business Strength:** You think in quarters. You move fast. You course-correct early.

**Wealth Blind Spot:** You evaluate decade-long strategies with month-to-month expectations. One down year makes you question the plan.

Long-term investments often look unimpressive in short windows and brilliant over decades. Pattern recognition gone wrong: you apply business decision cycles to investments that require patience.

# Why These Persist

These aren't character flaws or knowledge gaps. They're natural responses to the fundamental difference between building a business and building wealth.

In business, you learned that control creates success. Every detail you managed, every decision you made directly, every dollar you watched—it all mattered. That vigilance built your company. But in wealth building, that same vigilance becomes counterproductive. Markets reward patience over action, discipline over control.

The paradoxes persist because they once protected you. That liquidity hoarding? It saved you during the 2008 crisis when credit disappeared overnight. That control obsession? It prevented costly mistakes when you were learning. That reinvestment compulsion? It built the business that created your success.

---

**Your business needed your constant attention to survive its early years. Your wealth needs your strategic neglect to thrive over decades.**

---

The challenge isn't abandoning these instincts—they're part of what made you successful. It's recognizing when to apply them and when to set them aside. Your business needed your constant attention to survive its early years. Your wealth needs your strategic neglect to thrive over decades.

One owner put it perfectly: "I had to learn that my portfolio isn't sick when it's quiet." In business, silence means something's wrong. In investing, it means everything's working.

Understanding why these paradoxes exist—that they're features of your success, not bugs—makes it easier to work with them rather than against them.

## The Shift

Entrepreneurs who build personal wealth don't abandon their instincts. They just apply them differently. They still optimize—but they review investment fees annually instead of ignoring them. They still want control—but they control the process and timeline, not daily market movements. They still reinvest—but they reinvest a percentage in diversified assets, not everything back into operations.

The skills that built your company are valuable for wealth building—when you recognize which decisions need urgency and control, and which need time and discipline.

Understanding these paradoxes is the first step. You've already proven you can master complex challenges—building revenue, managing operations, creating profitable systems. The question is whether you'll apply that same capability to systematic wealth building—which requires a fundamentally different approach.

### KEY TAKEAWAY

The Entrepreneur's Paradox shows that the same instincts that power a company can also power personal wealth—once you know when to shift from urgency and control to patience and process.

| Owner's Checklist | | |
|---|---|---|
| **Metric to watch** | **Conversation to schedule** | **Action within 30 days** |
| Percent of personal cash earning < 1% (beyond 6-month runway) | Ask advisor to stress-test plan for a 50% business-value drop | With professional guidance, develop a plan for excess cash earning less than 1% |

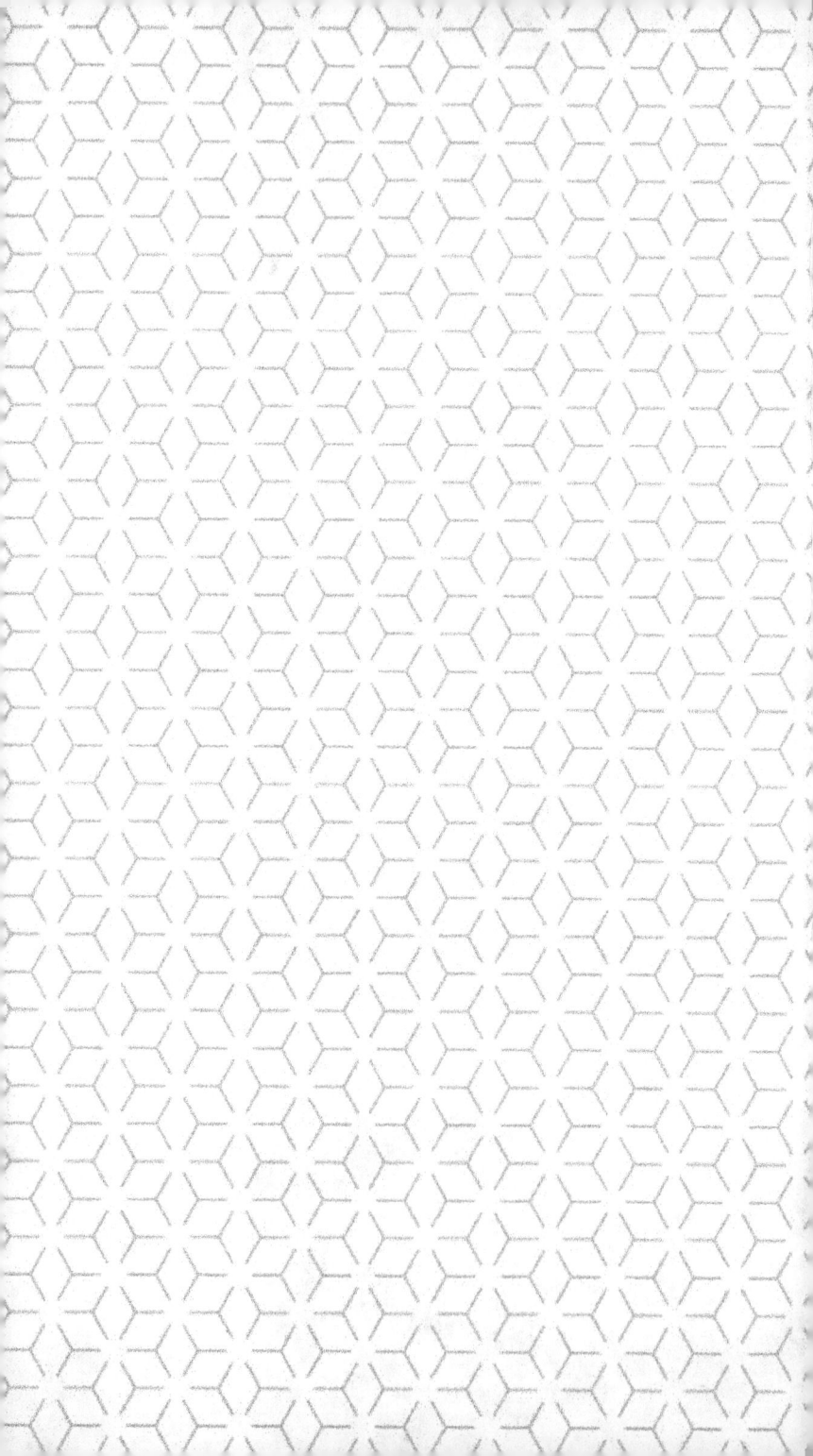

# PART II:
# THE PLANNING-
# FIRST SOLUTION

You've seen the gap. You understand the paradoxes. You know that systematic transfers can create unexpected value in both personal wealth and business operations. Now comes the question: How do you actually do this while running a demanding business?

The solution isn't higher returns or complex investments. It's not about working harder or waiting for the perfect exit. It's about building personal wealth systematically while you run the business, using the same discipline that makes companies valuable.

This section provides three essential elements: the mental shifts that make wealth building automatic, the coordination that multiplies value, and the strategies that work for owners—not employees.

The framework is deceptively simple: systematic transfers, coordinated planning, and the patience to let both compound. But simple doesn't mean easy. It requires thinking differently about the relationship between business success and personal wealth.

# CHAPTER 5

# THE MISSING 20 PERCENT: CONVERTING BUSINESS WINS INTO LASTING WEALTH

**M**y kids compete in tournament-level sports. They practice relentlessly, master technique, build strength and endurance. At tournaments, everyone is good. The winners find an extra 20 percent—the difference maker. I push for that margin because I know the effort behind it.

## Building Wealth That Lasts

Owners face a similar challenge. You've already done the 80 percent—the incredible work of building a successful business. You've mastered revenue generation, cash flow management, team building. You make payroll under pressure, navigate cash crunches, carry responsibility for dozens of families.

That's the heavy lifting. The hard part. The 80 percent that most people never achieve.

But then your money sits in cash with no strategy while everything else in your business runs with surgical precision. The missing 20 percent—systematically converting business success into personal wealth—is what separates owners who feel financially vulnerable despite their success from those who achieve genuine independence.

Think of it this way: Building your business was 80 percent of the journey—the hardest part. You've already done that. The missing 20 percent is taking what you've built and systematically converting it into personal wealth. Not more work. Just different application of the skills you already have.

---

## The missing 20 percent turns income into independence.

---

# Three Shifts

Successful owners who bridge this gap don't revolutionize everything at once. They make three fundamental shifts that unlock what they've already built:

## 1. Separation: Two Scorecards, Not One

Most owners measure everything by business performance. Good quarter equals security. Tough quarter equals stress. Your entire financial identity rides on last month's P&L.

> **The shift:** *Develop separate scorecards for business success and personal security. They're related but distinct, like revenue and profit—connected but requiring different strategies.*

The fear that holds owners back? They worry systematic transfers will weaken their business.

Chapter 3 showed how the commercial flooring owner's disciplined distributions increased his company's value. But separation matters for another reason too.

When your only measure of security is your business bank balance, every decision carries too much weight. Should you invest in new equipment or keep the cash? Hire that key person or preserve the cushion? You're not making strategic decisions—you're protecting your only safety net.

Once you have assets building outside the business, these become what they should be: business decisions, evaluated on business merits. Separation doesn't just build wealth. It clears your thinking.

## 2. Automation: From Negotiation to System

Every month, the same debate: Should I invest this month? How much? Maybe wait until next quarter when things are clearer?

> **The shift:** *Make wealth building automatic, not emotional. Set the system once, let it run.*

Many owners make the same wealth-building decision twelve times a year. Good months trigger debates about saving more. Tough months justify skipping transfers. Each decision burns mental energy better spent on strategic thinking.

The irony? You've already automated everything critical in your business. Payroll runs automatically. Inventory reorders at set levels. Subscriptions renew without thought. Yet the one transfer that builds your personal security—the one that pays you—requires monthly deliberation.

Automation isn't about the mechanics. It's about removing friction from progress. When transfers happen automatically, wealth building stops being a monthly negotiation with yourself and becomes as reliable as your other business systems.

Start conservatively—an amount you can maintain even in tough quarters. The specific amount matters less than breaking the pattern of monthly decision fatigue. Once you see the system working, increasing it becomes easy. But first, you need to stop treating your own wealth building as optional.

## 3. Progress Over Perfection

In business, you launched before you were ready. Hired before you had perfect candidates. Expanded before conditions were ideal. But with personal wealth, owners suddenly demand guarantees that don't exist.

> **The shift:** *Apply the same bias toward action that built your business. Starting imperfectly beats waiting for perfect conditions.*

The "what-ifs" become paralyzing. Market drops, cash needs, investment choices, better strategies— the search for certainty prevents any action at all.

Yet you're applying standards to wealth building that you'd never apply to business. You launched your company without perfect conditions. You made your first hire without guarantees. You knew that waiting for certainty meant never starting.

The same principle applies here. Start with half your target amount if that feels safer. Choose simple, diversified investments while you learn. Set up basic tax-advantaged accounts before optimizing every strategy.

The hardest part isn't the money—it's accepting that progress beats perfection. In business, you've learned that 70 percent execution beats 100 percent planning. Your wealth building deserves the same pragmatic approach.

Movement creates momentum. Start where you are, with what you have. You can optimize as you go—just like you did with everything else you've built.

## Visible Action vs. Invisible Growth

In business, effort often maps cleanly to outcomes. More qualified sales activity typically increases revenue. Tighter operations generally improve margins. The connection between action and result is visible, often immediate.

Wealth building feels different. The actions that create wealth—automatic transfers, patient investing, steady execution—work largely out of sight. Compound growth is invisible day-to-day, obvious only over years. The most powerful forces operate below your radar.

This disconnect explains why capable business owners struggle with wealth building. Business rewards visible action and quick pivots. Wealth rewards systematic patience and staying the course.

Chapter 4 explored how business owners naturally compare business returns to investment returns—missing that they serve entirely different purposes.

---

## Your business creates income. Your investments create security.

---

Once you stop comparing them, the resistance fades.

## The Compound Effect of Small Shifts

These three shifts—separation, automation, progress—seem minor individually. Together, they create something powerful.

Separation gives automation a purpose. You're not just moving money between accounts; you're building genuine independence from business volatility. Automation turns that purpose into reality without monthly deliberation. And progress—even modest progress—proves the system works, which makes you willing to separate more, automate more confidently, and trust the process instead of demanding perfection.

Each shift enables the next. More importantly, each shift makes the others easier to sustain.

We saw this pattern in chapter 3—the owner's systematic transfers inadvertently created the discipline that made his business more valuable. Research confirms that automated savings meaningfully increase wealth over time. But the real power isn't in any single shift. It's in how they reinforce each other, creating momentum that builds naturally.

The pattern is predictable. Year one feels uncomfortable because you're fighting your instincts. By year two, the system starts working with your business brain instead of against it. By year five, both your business and personal wealth have grown beyond what either would have achieved alone.

# Structure over Willpower

These shifts don't happen through willpower. They happen through structure.

Without a framework, every wealth decision becomes a debate. With one, wealth building becomes as systematic as your operations. That's the missing 20 percent—applying your existing brilliance to complete the wealth-building work you've already mostly done.

Next, we'll explore the Planning-First framework that makes these shifts automatic. But first, recognize this: You've built the engine. Now we're just directing some of its power toward securing your future.

## KEY TAKEAWAY

You've already completed 80% of the work by building a successful business. The missing 20%—systematic wealth building through separated scorecards, automated transfers, and progress over perfection—converts that business success into lasting personal wealth.

| Owner's Checklist | | |
| --- | --- | --- |
| Metric to watch | Conversation to schedule | Action within 30 days |

| Percent of monthly profit automatically routed to personal accounts | With key stakeholders: agree on a target auto-transfer (e.g., 10% of net profit) | Activate an automatic transfer for the next profit distribution—start with any sustainable amount |
| --- | --- | --- |

# CHAPTER 6

# PLANNING-FIRST IN PRACTICE

**M**ost business owners excel at business planning—forecasting revenue, managing cash flow, optimizing operations with intention and strategy.

But personal wealth often happens differently—moved to personal accounts when the business checking looks healthy, invested when someone makes a compelling pitch, optimized for taxes only when deadlines loom.

It's not lack of discipline but lack of system. You've systematized everything else in your business, but wealth building still runs on feel and timing rather than process and strategy.

Planning-First changes this. It applies the same systematic thinking you use for business operations to building personal wealth. Instead of hoping wealth follows business success, you create a system where they advance together.

## What Planning-First Means

Planning-First isn't about having more plans—every owner already has growth projections, exit timelines, and retirement dreams. Planning-First means creating a system where personal wealth building happens automatically alongside business operations.

> **Traditional approach:** Build the business, figure out wealth later.

> **Planning-First approach:** Build wealth systematically while running the business.

The difference shows up in how decisions get made. When you're buying equipment, you know the tax implications before signing. When cash flow surges, distributions happen automatically. When opportunities arise, you evaluate them against both business and personal metrics.

This isn't complex. It's a system with two components: a quarterly rhythm that prevents scrambles and integration points that connect business and personal finance. Once implemented, wealth building becomes as systematic as making payroll.

------------------------------------------------

## Planning-First means wealth building happens automatically alongside business operations, not hopefully after business success.

------------------------------------------------

## The Quarterly Rhythm

December tax scrambles happen because there's no system. The Planning-First framework spreads the work across four quarters, each with a specific focus:

**Q1 (January - March): Annual Planning** Start the year with strategy. Set your wealth-building targets for the year, review your entity structure for potential changes (remember, many elections like S-Corp must be filed by March 15 for calendar-year businesses), and establish your systematic transfer amounts. This quarter sets the foundation while you have clarity and time.

**Q2 (April - June): Post Tax Season Review**
Your CPA just spent weeks in your numbers, so capture insights while they're fresh. What worked last year? What didn't? What changes would improve this year?

This isn't about dwelling on the past but implementing lessons while you have time to execute. The S-Corp owner who paid too much in payroll tax adjusts their salary/distribution mix now—optimizing within reasonable compensation rules. The business that missed retirement funding deadlines sets up automatic contributions now (SEP-IRAs can still be funded through extension deadlines, but employee deferrals need different timing).

**Q3 (July - September): Midyear Calibration**
*This is your sweet spot—late enough to see patterns, early enough to change outcomes.*

Business changes constantly. Q3 compares reality to projections and adjusts accordingly. The manufacturer whose sales exceeded projections adjusts estimated taxes now to avoid penalties. The consultant whose major client departed reduces personal distributions before cash gets tight.

This is when smart tax planning happens. Model that equipment purchase now—Section 179 versus bonus depreciation, this year versus next. Evaluate pension options while there's time to implement. Start gifting strategies if a sale might be on the horizon (assignment-of-income rules care about timing).

**Q4 (October - December): Pre-Year-End Positioning** *Execute what you planned in Q3.*

October and November are for implementation—equipment purchases you've already modeled, retirement contributions you've already calculated, income timing you've already planned. The SECURE Act provides more flexibility on retirement plan adoption, but the real advantage comes from planning ahead, not rushing deadlines.

By December, you're implementing decisions you've already made, not discovering problems you should have addressed.

In reality, you'll hit maybe half these quarters in year one, more in year two. That's fine. The framework ensures nothing critical gets missed, even when business chaos takes precedence. The best advisors for business owners track this rhythm even when you can't. They know you'll miss quarters when deals close or crises hit. Their job is maintaining the framework so you meet year-end deadlines strategically—regardless of what November throws at you.

# The Four Integration Points

The quarterly rhythm creates discipline. Integration points create value. These four areas, when connected to your business operations, multiply wealth building automatically.

## Cash Flow Synchronization

Every business has patterns—seasonal surges, contract renewals, and predictable slow periods that repeat year after year. Yet most owners transfer money to personal accounts randomly, based on gut feel about the checking balance.

Planning-First aligns transfers with actual patterns. The agency with March and September contract renewals automates larger distributions in April and October. The retailer with strong Q4 sales schedules heavy transfers in January. The consultant with irregular project timing maintains steady monthly transfers at conservative levels.

The system runs automatically without monthly debates about whether to transfer, without guilt about taking "too much" during good months or regret about missing opportunities. The transfers match your business reality because you designed them that way.

One construction company mapped their cash patterns over two years, then automated transfers accordingly. In three years, this systematic approach moved mid-six figures to personal wealth—money that previously sat in business checking earning nothing, creating no security, building no independence.

## Tax Strategy Optimization

Your business structure creates opportunities—entity elections, retirement plan design, equipment timing, charitable strategies—but these only create value when integrated with business operations.

The S-Corp owner discovers their salary/distribution mix needs adjusting—but within reasonable compensation rules, as the IRS can reclassify distributions as wages if salary is too low. Finding the optimal balance saves thousands in payroll taxes while maintaining compliance.

The profitable company implements a defined benefit plan, creating significant deductions while securing retirement. But only because they evaluated it in Q2, not December. While retirement plan rules continue evolving (the SECURE Act expanded adoption deadlines), thoughtful design always requires lead time.

The real estate investor times improvements for maximum depreciation benefit. The manufacturer coordinates equipment purchases with current Section 179 and bonus depreciation rules. The consultant strategically bunches charitable deductions for optimal tax impact.

None of this is aggressive or complex. It's simply connecting tax strategy to business operations before decisions get made, not after.

## Risk Architecture

Many owners' protection is backward—heavy business insurance but minimal personal coverage. If something happens to you, the business might survive but your family struggles.

Planning-First flips this by establishing personal life insurance independent of business performance, disability coverage that replaces income (not just business overhead), and umbrella policies protecting wealth outside the company. Each piece reinforces the others instead of duplicating or leaving gaps.

The integration happens when you connect coverage to wealth building. As personal assets grow through systematic transfers, umbrella coverage increases. As business value rises, buy-sell agreements need updating (especially given evolving valuation rules). As retirement approaches, coverage shifts from protection to legacy.

Protection should match what you're building, not what you used to have.

## Strategic Timing

Timing multiplies value—not market timing but business timing. When you make moves is as important as what moves you make.

Start gifting strategies well before any sale discussions, not when buyers appear. The rules focus on whether a sale was "practically certain" at gift time, so planning years ahead beats rushing close to a deal. Implement retirement plans when they can compound for decades, not when you're trying to catch up. Model entity structure changes early in the year when you can still file elections, not when it's too late.

One owner began transferring nonvoting shares to children years before selling—small annual gifts at low valuations that accumulated significantly. By sale time, substantial wealth had transferred without tax impact, without losing control, and critically, without triggering assignment-of-income issues because the gifts happened well before any definitive agreement.

Another implemented a defined benefit plan at age forty-five instead of fifty-five, gaining ten extra years of compound growth and ten extra years of tax deductions—dramatically different outcomes.

Strategic timing means starting early enough that time works for you instead of against you.

## The System in Action

Watch how the Planning-First system handles a common scenario: major equipment purchase.

**Without the system:** December arrives and your CPA mentions you need deductions. You rush to buy equipment—maybe it's the right equipment, maybe not. Maybe it's the right timing, maybe not. The tax deduction drives the decision.

**With Planning-First:** Q2 identifies the equipment need, then Q3 models three scenarios—buy now, buy Q1, or lease instead. You evaluate cash flow impact, tax benefits, and business operations before making a strategic decision that gets implemented smoothly.

The same equipment and same tax deduction produce completely different outcomes because the system drove the process, not the deadline.

This plays out across every major decision. Expansion opportunities evaluated against both business and personal metrics. New hires timed with cash flow patterns. Exit planning started years early instead of months late.

# The Compound Effect

Year one feels different immediately because December rushes disappear and transfers happen automatically without constant decision-making.

Year two builds momentum as personal wealth grows and business decisions improve because personal stress decreases. The system starts working for you instead of you working the system.

Year three shows the full impact when business and personal wealth grow together, opportunities you would have missed get captured, and problems that would have been expensive get prevented.

The results vary by situation, but owners report spending significantly less time managing finances, meaningful tax savings, and building six-figure personal wealth by year three. But the transformation goes deeper than numbers. When wealth building becomes systematic, business ownership becomes sustainable.

## Starting Simple

You don't need to revolutionize everything at once. Start with two simple actions:

First, implement one quarter of the rhythm. If it's Q1, review last year's tax return and identify one improvement. If it's Q3, make one positioning move for year-end. Small starts build confidence.

Second, pick your highest-impact integration point. If cash flow is erratic, map your patterns and automate one transfer. If taxes surprise you annually, get your CPA and advisor on one thirty-minute call—watch what surfaces.

------------------------------------------------

**Without a framework, every wealth decision becomes a debate. With one, wealth building becomes as systematic as your operations.**

------------------------------------------------

The Planning-First system isn't complex—quarterly rhythm, four integration points. Once implemented, building wealth becomes as automatic as running your business.

## KEY TAKEAWAY

The Planning-First system—quarterly rhythm
plus integration points—makes wealth building as
systematic as your business operations. Business
success and personal wealth finally advance together.

| Owner's Checklist | | |
| --- | --- | --- |
| **Metric to watch** | **Conversation to schedule** | **Action within 30 days** |
| Which quarter you handle tax planning (goal: Q3, not Q4) | With your CPA: "What if we met in September instead of December?" | Schedule your first Q3 tax planning session— even 30 minutes |

# CHAPTER 7

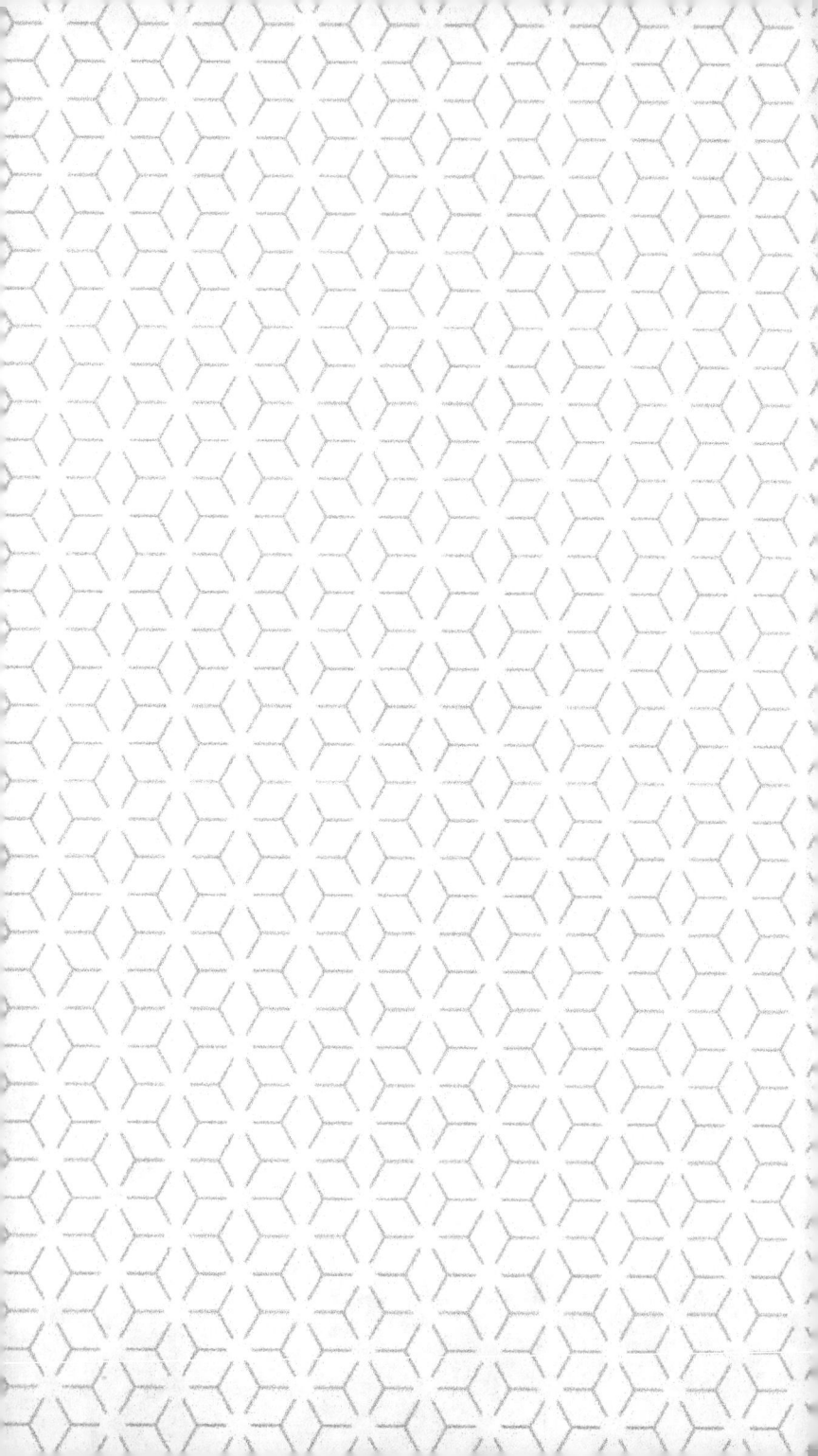

# WHY THE RULES ARE DIFFERENT FOR OWNERS

You ou control when you recognize income. You decide how to structure compensation. You can time major purchases, accelerate deductions, and design benefit programs. These aren't complications—they're advantages that employees never get.

Yet most financial planning treats these advantages as problems to solve rather than opportunities to leverage. Built for steady paychecks and predictable timelines, traditional frameworks miss the wealth-building power inherent in business ownership.

Your financial reality operates on different physics: irregular cash flow that would terrify most employees, concentrated equity that breaks every diversification rule, and a balance sheet that serves as both current income and future retirement. These aren't obstacles to work around—they're the exact features that, properly leveraged, create extraordinary wealth.

## Seven Differences

Understanding these distinctions explains why generic advice feels wrong and why integrated planning delivers what you actually need.

# The Owner's Advantage

| Area | Employee Reality | Owner Reality | The Opportunity |
|---|---|---|---|
| **Retirement Goals** | Age-based finish line at 65 | Freedom on your terms: phased exit, partial sale, advisory role | Design for optionality, not calendar dates |
| **Tax Strategy** | Year-end optimization | Quarterly entity + distribution decisions | Coordination **can save tens of thousands** annually |
| **Liquidity** | Wealth in liquid accounts | Wealth tied up in business equity | Build accessible wealth before you need it— concentration creates desperation |
| **Cash Flow** | Monthly paycheck, autoinvest | Variable/ seasonal income | **Match transfers to your business cycles for better results** |
| **Investment Risk** | Allocation by age | Risk concentrated in one business | Personal portfolio offsets—not duplicates—your business risk |
| **Exit Timeline** | Plan 3-5 years before retirement | Start 5-10 years while thriving | Early preparation means **you set terms rather than accept them** |
| **Planning Scope** | Investment management | **Business, tax, estate, exit coordination** | Integrated planning captures value hiding between professional silos |

## Retirement: Building Freedom, Not Hitting Dates

Employees circle a date on the calendar—the day they stop working. You're building something different: the freedom to choose your involvement level. Maybe that's stepping back to advisory, selling partially, or transitioning seasonally. Success isn't reaching sixty-five; it's having options at forty-five, fifty-five, or whenever life priorities shift.

This fundamental difference reshapes planning entirely. Instead of calculating withdrawal rates for a specific date, you're creating multiple income streams that work independently. Instead of binary retirement planning, you're building transition flexibility that lets you dial involvement up or down based on interest, not necessity.

## Tax Strategy: Quarterly Coordination, Not Yearly Filing

Employees optimize what they're given—max the 401(k), take standard deductions, file in April. You operate in a different universe with controllable variables that employees can't access.

You decide salary versus distributions, choosing the optimal mix within reasonable compensation rules. You time income recognition, accelerating or deferring based on tax brackets. You select retirement structures—SEP, Solo 401(k), defined benefit—based on current cash flow and future needs. Each decision shapes not just this year's taxes but your long-term wealth trajectory.

The complexity creates opportunity. Coordinating entity structure, distribution timing, and retirement contributions throughout the year routinely saves business owners five figures annually. But it requires thinking beyond the December rush to year-round strategy where every quarter's decisions align with your complete financial picture.

## Liquidity: Accessible Wealth Beyond Business Equity

Up to 80 percent of your net worth might be locked in business equity—valuable on paper, inaccessible in reality. A downturn hits twice: reducing current income while eroding total net worth. You can't tap business equity like employees access their 401(k).

Building liquidity outside the business is not lacking faith in your company. It is creating flexibility that strengthens your business decisions. When personal wealth exists independently, you make strategic choices rather than desperate ones. You can wait for the right buyer rather than accepting the first offer. You can invest in growth without risking personal security.

The systematic transfers that build personal liquidity don't weaken your business—they create the stability that enables better long-term decisions.

## Cash Flow: Rhythms, Not Regularity

Automated investing works brilliantly for employees with predictable paychecks. Your reality is different—seasonal surges, project-based revenue, quarterly distributions that vary with business performance.

Fighting against these patterns with forced monthly contributions creates unnecessary stress. Working with them creates superior results. A landscaping business that contributes heavily from April through September and reduces in winter captures more wealth than forcing equal monthly amounts. A consultant who ties transfers to project completions builds more than attempting steady contributions.

The key is designing rules that adapt: "Transfer 20 percent of any month exceeding target revenue" or "Contribute quarterly distributions above operating reserves." These systems work because they align with how your business generates cash.

## Investment Allocation: Balancing Concentrated Risk

Traditional allocation models assume your risk comes from your portfolio. Yours comes from your business—a single, concentrated, economy-sensitive asset that represents most of your net worth.

If you own hotels, you already have exposure to travel trends, season occupancy, and economic cycles. Adding hospitality stocks to your portfolio doubles down on the same risks. If your tech company thrives in growth markets, your personal portfolio might need defensive positions to balance total exposure.

Your business is part of your asset allocation, not separate from it. Personal investments should complement, not duplicate, your business risk profile.

## Timeline Planning: Early Preparation, Maximum Leverage

Employees can decide to retire with a few years' notice. Your transition requires five to ten years of preparation to optimize value and terms. Buyers want clean financials, demonstrated systems, and transferable operations—none of which develop overnight.

Starting early means being ready when opportunities emerge. The owner who begins succession planning while the business is thriving has leverage. The one who waits until burnout or health issues force a sale has none.

Early preparation—building systems, developing management, creating transferable value—makes you exit-optional rather than exit-desperate. This shift in leverage can mean millions in additional sale proceeds.

## Planning Scope: Integration over Isolation

Employee planning is primarily investment management—asset allocation, rebalancing, performance monitoring. Your planning touches everything: entity structure, tax strategy, business operations, personal wealth, exit preparation, estate design, family legacy.

These elements interconnect in ways that siloed advice misses. A distribution strategy that optimizes taxes might compromise loan qualification. An entity structure that protects assets might limit retirement contributions. A succession plan that maximizes value might create estate tax problems.

You need professionals who see these connections and coordinate accordingly, not just managing investments but optimizing the complete system.

# Why Integration Multiplies Value

One landscaping business owner discovered this firsthand. Traditional advice pushed steady monthly contributions that ignored seasonal reality. Winter months meant stress about funding accounts while summer excess cash sat idle.

The shift to integrated planning transformed the approach. Contributions now range from minimal in January through March to three to four times that amount in peak season. The same business cash flow now builds more wealth with less stress—not through complicated strategies but through simple alignment with business reality.

This pattern repeats across every difference. Tax strategies that save tens of thousands. Exit preparation that adds millions to sale value. Investment allocation that reduces total risk while improving returns. Each element compounds when coordinated rather than isolated.

-----------------------------------------------

**The systematic transfers that build wealth create more business value than keeping every dollar inside ever could.**

-----------------------------------------------

## From Isolation to Integration

These seven differences aren't complications to overcome—they're advantages to leverage. When planning aligns with owner reality rather than fighting it, wealth building becomes systematic rather than sporadic.

Your CPA optimizes taxes but may not see wealth strategy. Your attorney protects assets but might not understand exit timing. Your banker wants growth but doesn't factor in personal security. They're each solving their piece without seeing your complete picture.

Integrated planning connects these pieces, not through complex strategies but through coordination that captures opportunities hiding in the gaps between professional silos.

---

**Business owners live by different financial rules—irregular income, concentrated equity, controllable timing. Integrated planning turns those differences into systematic wealth-building advantages.**

---

Next, we'll explore why certain owners naturally embrace this integrated approach while others resist—and why both types ultimately need the same systematic framework to convert business success into lasting wealth.

## KEY TAKEAWAY

The seven critical differences between employee and owner finances aren't obstacles—they're opportunities. Integrated planning that acknowledges these differences and coordinates across them creates wealth that siloed advice never could.

| Owner's Checklist: Leveraging Your Differences | | |
|---|---|---|
| **Metric to watch** | **Conversation to schedule** | **Action within 30 days** |
| Number of the 7 owner advantages you actively use today | With your advisor: "How do we capture the opportunities I'm missing as an owner vs. employee?" | Pick one owner advantage to implement: liquidity (set first transfer), tax timing (schedule Q3 planning), or cash flow alignment (map your seasonal patterns) |

# CHAPTER 8

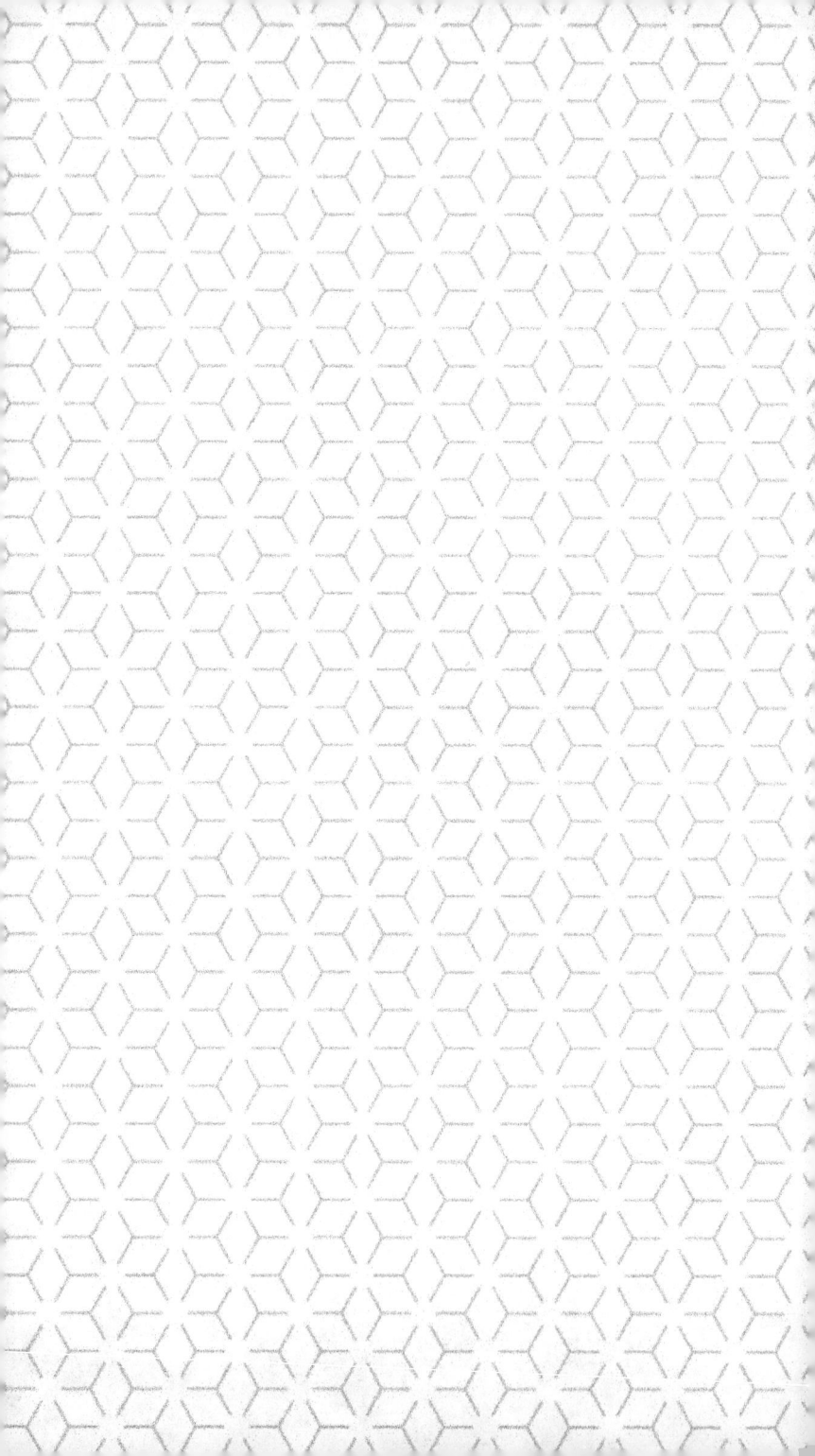

# WHY OWNERS ENGAGE

**M**ost business owners don't resist financial planning. They resist planning that doesn't fit how they operate.

When advisors use employee frameworks for entrepreneurs, separate investment management from business strategy, or can't explain how personal wealth connects to business cycles—that's not resistance to planning. That's recognizing a mismatch.

Owners generally fall into two categories based on their experiences and what they're seeking. Understanding which type you are explains why certain approaches resonate while others don't.

## Two Types of Owners

These owners have usually worked with advisors before. They have investment accounts, maybe a SEP-IRA, some life insurance. But something fundamental is missing—coordination.

They've watched their CPA optimize business taxes while their investment advisor operates in complete isolation. They've seen their attorney structure business entities without anyone considering the personal wealth implications. Every professional handles their slice, but nobody sees the complete picture.

One S-Corp owner discovered an opportunity his advisor hadn't explored—optimizing his salary-versus-distribution mix could save thousands in payroll taxes while maintaining retirement contributions. They'd been working together for three years, but without coordination between entity structure and investment planning, this tax-saving strategy had been overlooked.

These owners aren't looking for another investment manager. They're looking for someone who understands that business and personal finances are inseparable for entrepreneurs.

## The Control Seekers

Control seekers often manage their own investments successfully. A construction company owner might pick stocks based on industry knowledge—buying equipment manufacturers before infrastructure booms, loading up on building supply companies when demand rises. The track record might be impressive.

The concern about working with an advisor comes from the fear that someone will try to take over, push index funds, or make them feel foolish for active trading.

But these owners also recognize they need something more systematic for retirement, something that doesn't depend on the next good pick. The approach that works doesn't try to eliminate their trading—it builds systematic wealth alongside it. They keep their trading account while systematic strategies build core wealth. They keep control where they want it while delegating what they don't want to manage.

# The Universal Gap

Despite different experiences, both types of owners want the same things from financial planning. The disconnect between what they want and what they typically get explains why so many successful business owners have fragmented financial lives.

### What Owners Want vs. What They Often Get

| What Owners Want | What They Often Get |
|---|---|
| **Structure & Process**<br>Clear road map, systematic approach, visual progress tracking | Disjointed meetings, unclear methodology, no connection to business operations |
| **Coordination**<br>Business, tax, and personal wealth integrated | Investment products without strategy; advice in silos |
| **Control & Transparency**<br>Ability to delegate or stay hands-on, with full visibility | "Trust us, we've got it" —no operational clarity |
| **Appropriate Timelines**<br>Reviews and metrics paced to business cycles | Generic "think long-term" reminders that ignore quarterly rhythms |
| **Sophisticated Simplicity**<br>Complex strategies explained simply, not dumbed down | Either patronizing oversimplification OR unnecessary complexity |
| **Business Understanding**<br>Advisor who understands operations and owner mindset | Employee-focused advice with business owner pricing |

This gap isn't about advisors lacking expertise. It's about an industry built for one type of client trying to serve another. The frameworks, timelines, and strategies that work perfectly for employees with steady paychecks don't translate to the reality of business ownership.

---

**Business owners don't resist planning. They resist planning that doesn't fit how they operate.**

---

## When the Approach Matches the Owner

The shift happens when owners find planning that works like their business does—systematic, coordinated, and built for them.

A software developer had been investing for years, receiving quarterly performance reports, but something was missing. No one had ever looked at how his business and personal finances worked together. His investments existed in one world, his business in another, and his tax planning in a third. Each piece was professionally managed, but no one was connecting the dots.

When he found an approach that requested everything—business financials, personal statements, tax returns—to see the complete picture, he had it organized and uploaded within days. He approached it like he would a bank loan application, recognizing the value of comprehensive analysis.

The assessment revealed opportunities hiding in the gaps: how entity structure and investment planning could work together, how business cash flow patterns could inform financial timing, and how tax strategies could be coordinated across both business and personal. For the first time, his complete financial reality became one integrated system rather than separate pieces.

He wasn't resistant to planning. He'd been waiting for someone to look at the whole picture.

## Business Instincts as Planning Assets

The right approach doesn't fight your business instincts—it channels them.

The need for control becomes systematic oversight of the whole picture. The optimization mindset shifts from timing markets to coordinating tax strategies. Strategic thinking builds long-term wealth architecture instead of chasing quarterly returns.

These instincts that some see as obstacles can become advantages when properly channeled:

**Control becomes valuable oversight of systematic strategies.** You're not giving up control; you're controlling the system rather than individual transactions.

**Action bias transforms into systematic processes**—scheduled quarterly reviews, strategic rebalancing based on thresholds, tax-loss harvesting. Activity with purpose rather than motion without progress.

**The optimization drive shifts to what matters**—fees, taxes, and coordination rather than trying to beat the market.

In business, when you have a bad year, you pivot. That responsiveness creates success. In investing, down years require staying the course—which feels wrong to every business instinct. The right approach doesn't try to eliminate these instincts but helps you recognize when to apply which mindset.

## The Pattern of Success

Owners who successfully build wealth alongside their businesses share common patterns:

They find planning that respects their need for control while providing systematic execution. They work with professionals who see business and personal wealth as interconnected, not separate. They implement systems that work with business cycles rather than against them.

Most importantly, they stop trying to force their financial lives into frameworks built for employees. Instead, they embrace planning designed for the reality of business ownership—variable income, concentrated risk, and the constant balance between business investment and personal security.

---

## The owners who successfully build wealth aren't the ones who abandon their instincts. They're the ones who find planning that works with how they think.

---

This is planning that fits how owners operate—not because it's special or complex, but because it's built for your reality instead of someone else's.

Next, we'll explore how this planning adapts through the natural cycles every business faces—because wealth building for owners isn't a straight line but a rhythm that matches your business seasons.

## KEY TAKEAWAY

Successful wealth building happens when owners
stop trying to fit into employee frameworks and find
planning that respects their instincts, coordinates their
complete picture, and works with their business reality.

| Owner's Checklist | | |
|---|---|---|
| **Metric to watch** | **Conversation to schedule** | **Action within 30 days** |
| Number of gaps between what you want and what you're getting (from the table) | With your current advisor or self: "Which planning gaps are costing me the most?" | Fix one gap— either add coordination, increase control, or align timelines with your business |

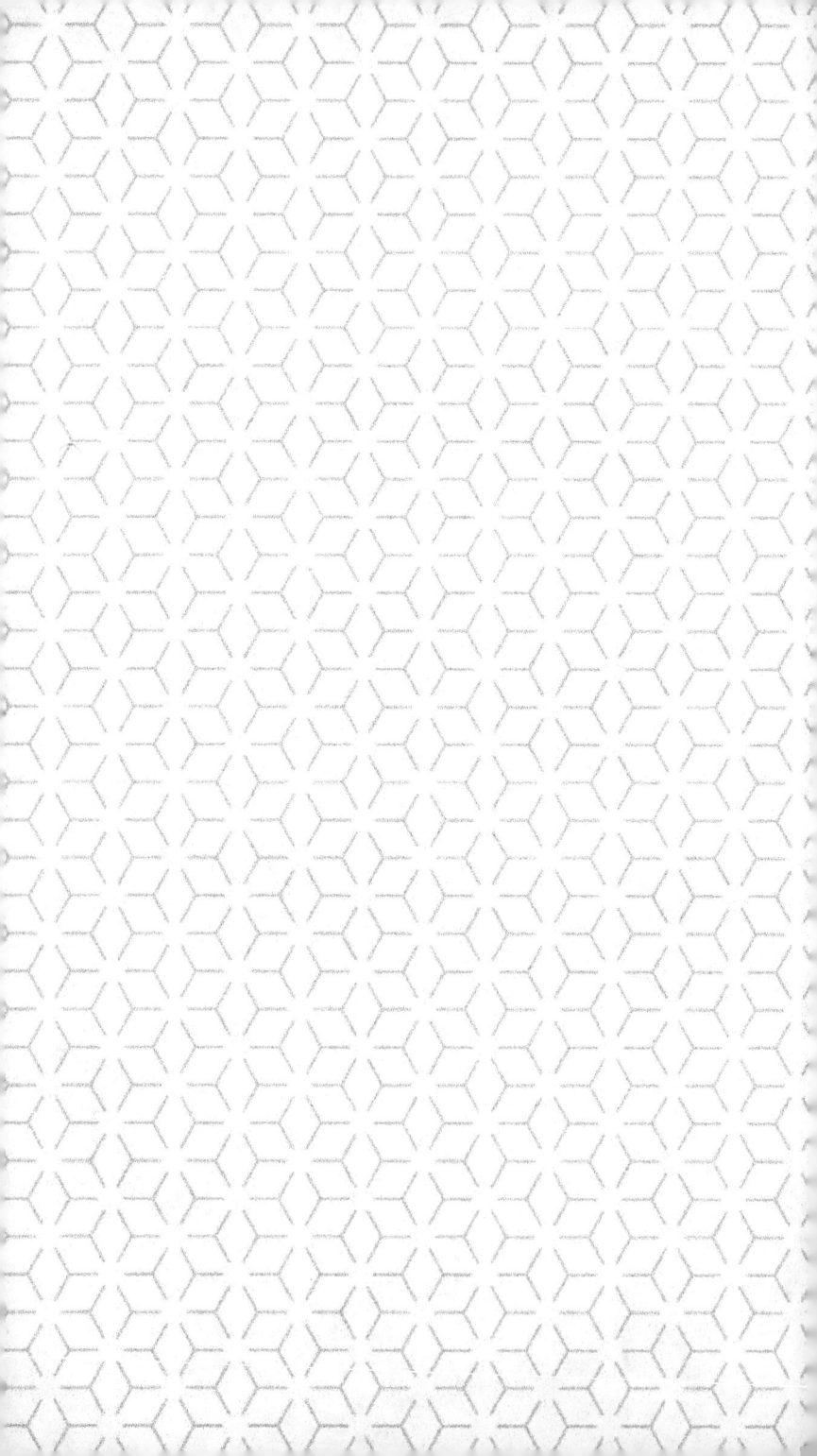

# PART III: IMPLEMENTATION

Part III shows how Planning-First works through real business cycles. You'll see what implementation looks like, how to maintain momentum through ups and downs, and why systematic wealth building strengthens both your business and personal finances.

The shift from reacting to building happens through practical steps that work with your business, not against it.

# CHAPTER 9

# CYCLE-PROOF
# WEALTH PLANNING

Your Planning-First system has been running for two years. You've built confidence in the approach, integrated it with your business operations, and started seeing meaningful progress toward wealth goals.

Then your biggest client offers a three-year contract worth twice your annual revenue. The opportunity requires hiring twelve people, leasing new facilities, and managing implementation across multiple locations. For the next eight months, you're working eighty-hour weeks making decisions that affect dozens of families.

What surprises most owners: Your financial planning doesn't add to the stress. Instead, there's relief.

The clarity of knowing your personal financial security operates independently of business performance lets you focus completely on capturing the opportunity. This isn't just planning that adapts to business cycles—it's planning that creates the mental space to lead from strength rather than anxiety.

## The Business Owner's Reality

The same quality that drives business success— total focus on immediate priorities—creates challenges for traditional planning approaches that assume regular engagement and consistent decision-making capacity.

When crisis hits your business, you don't think about portfolio rebalancing. You think about payroll, customers, and operational continuity. When major opportunities emerge, you don't consider retirement account optimization. You focus on capturing growth and managing expansion.

This is business reality. Yet most owners try to pause wealth building during crisis and accelerate it during growth. They have it backwards.

Crisis is when you most need the discipline of systematic transfers—it forces operational efficiency. Growth is when you're most tempted to abandon discipline—right when lifestyle creep and overconfidence peak.

# The Four Seasons of Business

Every business cycles through predictable seasons. Understanding them—and how wealth planning works through each—is the difference between building lasting wealth and constantly starting over.

## The Four Business Seasons

| Season | Business Focus | Planning Benefit |
|---|---|---|
| High Growth | New contracts, rapid hiring, scaling systems | Automated contributions prevent wealth neglect and lifestyle creep |
| Crisis Management | Customer loss, key departures, economic shocks | Separate personal wealth enables clearer business decisions |

| | | |
|---|---|---|
| Operational Excellence | Process improvement, margin tuning, systematizing | No urge to tinker with investments; optimization energy stays focused |
| Strategic Planning | Expansion, succession, exit strategy | Bandwidth for sophisticated moves because basics run automatically |

## High Growth Periods

Growth creates its own challenges. One business expanded into three new markets over two years. Cash was tight throughout the expansion, but systematic contributions continued automatically. The owner never questioned whether he was doing the right thing financially—he could focus entirely on execution knowing personal wealth building was handled.

This systematic approach prevents a common trap: lifestyle creep disguised as business rewards. When revenue surges, it's tempting to celebrate with "justified" purchases—upgraded offices, luxury travel that's "partially business," personal items that become "business expenses."

Having automated wealth building makes these decisions conscious rather than accidental. You're not accidentally consuming your wealth-building capacity during your most profitable periods.

## Crisis Management

A manufacturing business faced significant setback when regulatory changes eliminated one of their product lines. Because they had built personal wealth separate from the business, they had the creditworthiness to finance equipment to develop a new product line to replace the lost revenue. The owner could focus on solving the business problem instead of worrying about personal finances.

That clarity helped make better decisions faster. Without personal financial stress clouding judgment, strategic pivots become clearer. You're solving problems with business solutions, not rushing to protect personal security.

## When Technology Disrupts Your Model

Disruption doesn't arrive as abstract threat—it shows up as real pressure in real time.

A logistics company faced this when competitors adopted routing software that made their dispatcher-and-whiteboard system obsolete. The instinct: halt personal transfers, pour everything into upgrades. Instead, the owner maintained their 10 percent transfer and secured a business line of credit.

Having personal wealth growing actually improved loan terms. The bank saw stability, not desperation. The technology upgrade happened faster than if they'd tried to self-fund through stopping wealth transfers.

Another business watched automation eliminate a third of what their professional services team did. Rather than panic and stop distributions, they moved upmarket—focusing on strategic work computers can't replicate. The systematic transfers never stopped during eighteen months of repositioning.

The pattern is predictable: technology threatens your model, you feel pressure to abandon wealth building. But owners who thrive maintain discipline precisely because disruption is permanent, not temporary. There will always be another technology requiring capital. Building personal wealth during these changes—not after—creates stability for strategic decisions rather than survival reactions.

---

## Crisis is when you most need the discipline of systematic transfers. Growth is when you're most tempted to abandon it.

---

## Operational Excellence

During periods of operational focus, the temptation is to optimize everything—including investments. But having systematic wealth building removes this temptation. You channel optimization energy where it creates most value—in your business—while financial strategy benefits from consistent execution rather than constant adjustment.

The freed mental bandwidth proves invaluable. Instead of second-guessing investment decisions or timing markets, you're focused on operational improvements that directly impact profitability. Wealth building continues automatically in the background.

## Strategic Planning

When business owners clarify personal financial needs, strategic planning improves. One owner determined his retirement number during a planning period. Knowing what he actually needed helped evaluate whether to expand for additional value and informed his eventual exit strategy.

Working backward from personal needs to business value reshapes the entire strategy—growth plans, operational improvements, even potential buyer profiles. Personal clarity forces business strategy conversations that might otherwise drift indefinitely.

# The Exit Planning Reality

According to the Exit Planning Institute, only 20-30 percent of businesses that go to market successfully sell. More telling: while 99 percent of owners agree transition strategy is important, 80 percent have no written plans, and 50 percent have done no planning at all.[1]

---

1 Exit Planning Institute, State of Owner Readiness, accessed June 2025, https://exit-planning-institute.org/state-of-owner-readiness.

The primary reason for failure? Owners are unprepared. They believe exit planning is something you do eighteen to twenty-four months before selling, like preparing a house for market. But as industry experts note, "an exit strategy is a business strategy"—requiring years of advance preparation.

Most owners who fail to exit successfully never separated personal financial security from business performance. When 80 percent of your net worth is tied up in the business, you can't evaluate offers objectively or afford the time needed to maximize value.

This is why systematic personal wealth planning triggers better exit planning. When owners clarify personal financial needs, they naturally ask: "What does my business need to be worth? When might I need liquidity? How do I maximize transferable value?"

## What Systematic Payment Creates

Businesses that pay their owners consistently share common characteristics.

To pay yourself systematically, you can't be the business. You must build systems generating profit without constant presence. You must create predictable cash flow through seasonality. You must maintain clean separation between business and personal finances.

These aren't just good practices—they're exactly what makes businesses valuable to others. Systematic distributions require what buyers value: predictable profits, clean operations, owner independence. The transfers aren't about exit planning, but if you ever choose to sell, you'll discover you've been building transferable value all along.

---

**The systematic transfers that build personal wealth create exactly what buyers value: predictable profits and owner independence.**

---

## The Bottom Line

Businesses that thrive through every cycle share one characteristic: their owners' personal wealth strategies don't compete with business demands. The systematic approach works precisely because it doesn't require attention when your business needs it most.

Your business will always cycle through growth, crisis, excellence, and planning. The question is whether your wealth building will survive these cycles or surrender to them.

The answer lies in building systems that work through every season—not despite them but because of them. When wealth building becomes as systematic as payroll, it survives everything your business faces.

## KEY TAKEAWAY

Business cycles are predictable—growth, crisis, excellence, planning—and they'll repeat throughout ownership. Wealth planning that works through these rhythms rather than against them is the difference between building lasting wealth and constantly starting over.

| Owner's Checklist | | |
|---|---|---|
| **Metric to watch** | **Conversation to schedule** | **Action within 30 days** |
| Are your systematic transfers still running regardless of business season? | With yourself: "What would make me stop or skip transfers— and how do I prevent that?" | Identify your current season and set one specific protection to maintain transfers through it |

# CHAPTER 10

# INSIDE THE PLANNING PROCESS

Y ou've implemented Planning-First with systems running and transfers happening automatically. So why doesn't it feel like winning?

Most owners review progress after eighteen months expecting what they see in business—dramatic growth, clear victories, immediate feedback. Instead they find net worth growing steadily but quietly, tax bills lower but not eliminated, retirement projections on track but not spectacular.

"This is it?" they wonder. "This is what systematic planning delivers?"

Yes. And understanding why this feels different is crucial to recognizing when Planning-First is working effectively.

## Why Success Feels Different

Business owners measure progress through action and visible results. Wealth building works differently—progress happens through consistency and time, not intensity and effort.

In business, you know you're winning when everyone's talking about it. In wealth building, you know you're winning when you stop thinking about it.

This disconnect between how success feels in business versus wealth building explains why many owners abandon working systems, mistaking quiet progress for no progress.

------------------------------------------------

**In business, you know you're winning when everyone's talking about it. In wealth building, you know you're winning when you stop thinking about it.**

------------------------------------------------

# The Four Phases of Implementation

Wealth building unfolds predictably across four distinct phases. Understanding what happens in each phase helps you recognize progress when it's occurring.

## The Implementation Journey

| Phase | Timeline | Key Milestones |
|-------|----------|----------------|
| Foundation Building | Year 1 | Systems and accounts go live. First systematic transfers prove the business can pay consistently. Surprising discoveries emerge—goals often closer than expected. |
| Systems + Psychology | Years 2-3 | Personal decisions stop tracking business mood. Professional coordination becomes seamless. Stakeholders align on shared goals. Spending becomes intentional. |
| Strategic Confidence | Years 3-5+ | True optionality emerges. You work because you choose to. Negotiations become objective. Business grows more valuable as transfers prove independence. |
| Full Independence | Years 5+ | Business is most valuable when you need it least. Exit becomes choice, not necessity. You've built the ultimate asset—a business that funds life without consuming it. |

## Phase 1: Foundation Building (Year 1)

The foundation phase reveals unexpected opportunities. One couple discovered they could retire five years earlier than assumed once they mapped actual numbers instead of guesses.

The most labor-intensive part is initial setup—gathering documents, consolidating accounts, establishing systems. Some owners start with a portion of assets first to see the process work, then consolidate additional accounts as value becomes clear.

A dental practice owner discovered that implementing a 401(k) with profit-sharing could solve hygienist retention while tripling retirement contributions—connecting two problems he'd been solving separately.

## Phase 2: Systems + Psychology (Years 2-3)

Systems from phase 1 reshape behavior naturally. Personal financial decisions stop tracking business performance. Your professionals coordinate rather than operating in isolation. Tax planning happens year-round.

Planning brings couples together around shared goals. One couple described themselves as financial opposites—one frugal, one spending freely. With clear goals and automatic systems, spending became thoughtful while savings anxiety decreased because both could see progress.

## Phase 3: Strategic Confidence (Years 3-5+)

This phase delivers genuine options. A family business received an unexpected acquisition offer. Because personal finances no longer depended on exit proceeds, they evaluated objectively. When terms weren't right, they walked away. Six months later, better terms appeared.

Your unrealistic goals start getting calendar dates. The vacation home, sabbatical, passion project— they shift from someday to specific timelines. Not because you're earning more, but because you're building systematically.

## Phase 4: Full Independence (Years 5+)

Your business becomes most valuable precisely when you need it least. The wealth system runs without constant attention, like the business you built to operate without you.

Owners reaching this phase often want their children experiencing the same systematic approach. The ultimate achievement isn't the number—it's optionality. You can sell, keep running, or step back to advisory. Every choice becomes possible because none are necessary.

---

**You've built the ultimate asset—a business that funds life without consuming it.**

---

## Boring Progress

The most effective wealth-building strategies—systematic saving, tax-loss harvesting, strategic rebalancing—sound boring because they are boring. Their power comes from repetition, not innovation.

Consider what compounds over time:

- Tax-loss harvesting turning market drops into tax deductions

- Asset location—placing investments in the most tax-efficient accounts
- Annual tax savings invested instead of spent
- Autoescalating contributions that increase without you thinking about it
- Staying invested through market cycles instead of panic-selling
- Risk reduction from proper insurance preventing one catastrophic loss

None of these feel significant in the moment. All of them compound into significance.

------------------------------------------------

# The most effective wealth-building strategies are boring. Their power comes from repetition, not innovation.

------------------------------------------------

The shift happens gradually, then suddenly. One day you realize you haven't checked your business bank balance in months. A major client loss would be disappointing, not devastating. Your spouse suggests a vacation without asking "can we afford it?"

These aren't dramatic moments. They're the quiet signs that systematic wealth building is working exactly as designed.

Business rewards urgency—first to market, quick pivots, immediate action. Wealth rewards patience—compound growth, tax efficiency over time, market cycles playing out.

This creates cognitive dissonance for owners. Every business instinct says "make something happen." Every wealth principle says "let the system work."

The resolution comes from recognizing you're playing two different games simultaneously. In business, you're the active player. In wealth building, you're the patient investor. Both roles are essential. Neither works using the other's rules.

## Moving Forward

This progression from financial dependence to genuine independence happens predictably but quietly through four phases, each building on the last. When wealth building feels boring, the system is usually functioning exactly as designed.

This quiet progress creates something bigger than wealth. It transforms not just your finances but your relationship with the business itself. Next, we'll see what this complete transformation looks like—when the Owner's Dividend delivers not just money but genuine freedom.

## KEY TAKEAWAY

Success in wealth building feels different from business success—steady and systematic rather than dramatic and immediate. The journey unfolds in four predictable phases over 5+ years, each building on the last. When it feels boring, it's usually working.

| Owner's Checklist | | |
|---|---|---|
| **Metric to watch** | **Conversation to schedule** | **Action within 30 days** |
| Months since you checked business accounts before making personal decisions | With those involved in your financial life: "What decisions do we now make without checking the business bank account first?" | List three financial decisions you made this month without business panic—proof the system works |

# CHAPTER 11

# BEYOND SURVIVAL MODE

Y ou've built a successful business. You've implemented systematic wealth building. The Planning-First approach has been running for years. Now something fundamental shifts—you stop managing from scarcity and start leading from strength.

This goes beyond numbers on statements. When personal wealth operates independently of business performance, your decision-making, leadership, and even your definition of success transform.

# The Three Transformations

## Personal: From Reactive to Strategic

For twenty years, a business owner filtered every decision through immediate financial need; which projects to take, clients to pursue, equipment to buy—all driven by cash requirements rather than strategic fit.

After three years of systematic wealth building, the decision framework shifted completely. Turning down a large project that would have consumed the team for six months became possible because it didn't align with the move toward higher-margin work. Five years earlier, cash flow needs would have made that decision impossible.

Personal wealth security removes the desperation that undermines strategic thinking. You stop taking every project that generates revenue. You stop hiring whoever's available rather than waiting for the right fit. You stop solving today's problem in ways that create tomorrow's complications.

## Business: Building What Buyers Want without Trying

The discipline of paying yourself systematically transforms your business into exactly what buyers dream of finding—not because you're building to sell, but because a business that funds your life without consuming it is the definition of valuable.

Think about what systematic transfers require:

- Systems generating profit without your daily involvement
- Operations running whether you're present or not
- Clean separation between business and personal finances
- Predictable cash flow through ups and downs

These aren't just good practices—they're exactly what makes businesses valuable to others.

After five years of systematic transfers, one business had a routine valuation come back 40 percent higher than the last assessment. The valuer specifically noted: "Strong systematic operations, clean financials, demonstrated ability to generate consistent profits independent of owner involvement."

The owner hadn't been building for exit but for life. Yet a business that works for your life is the business everyone wants to buy.

---

**A business that funds your life without consuming it is the definition of a valuable business.**

---

## Leadership: From Scarcity to Strength

Your team doesn't just hear what you say—they feel how you operate. When personal finances create background stress, leadership becomes reactive and controlling. When you have genuine wealth independence, leadership transforms.

The shift shows in subtle ways: less micromanaging of routine decisions, more effective delegation because every choice doesn't carry personal financial weight, investing in employee development and systems rather than managing for immediate returns.

When personal wealth reaches the point where a bad quarter won't affect family security, that buffer doesn't create carelessness—it creates strategic thinking.

It also creates generosity. Once personal pressure lifts, owners often start investing differently in their communities—sponsoring youth sports, funding technical training, giving employees paid volunteer time.

The unexpected return: Customer loyalty deepens. Recruiting improves. The best employees stay longer. Personal wealth doesn't make owners more selfish—it often makes them more generous. And generosity, counterintuitively, strengthens business.

## The Complete Owner's Dividend

The systematic transfer from business to personal wealth—the Owner's Dividend—extends far beyond money moving between accounts. It delivers three distinct types of compounding returns:

## Financial Dividends (Immediate and Measurable)

- The systematic transfer itself building personal wealth
- Tax savings from coordinated strategies
- Compound growth happening automatically
- Stronger negotiating position with lenders and buyers
- Reduced cost of capital when you're not desperate

## Strategic Dividends (Emerging over Time)

- Ability to walk away from bad deals
- Decisions based on strategy rather than survival
- Readiness for opportunities whenever they arise
- Patience for the right buyer, terms, or timing
- Capacity to invest in long-term value over short-term cash

## Personal Dividends (Transforming Everything Else)

- Mental space freed from money worry
- Aligned goals with your spouse
- Confidence modeled for your children
- Leadership from strength rather than fear
- Generosity that builds community and loyalty

These dividends compound on each other. Financial security improves strategic decisions. Better decisions increase business value. Higher value creates more options. More options reduce stress. Less stress improves leadership. Better leadership drives growth. Growth funds more wealth building.

---

**Real wealth isn't about what you can buy; it's about what you can walk away from.**

---

## The Decision Only You Can Make

When personal wealth operates independently of business performance, owners face an unexpected challenge: defining what it all means.

You can hire professionals to manage investments, optimize taxes, structure estates. You can delegate operations and automate systems. But one decision can't be delegated: defining what your wealth is actually for.

Remember those three questions from chapter 2: "What is enough?" "What comes after?" "What if I had to stop?" The systematic transfers haven't just been moving money—they've been forcing you to answer: What am I building toward? What does enough look like? What legacy matters beyond balances?

The owners who thrive after business don't just have wealth—they have clarity about its purpose. That clarity requires the same leadership that built your business, now applied to designing your life.

# What Independence Looks Like

For business owners, wealth isn't about what you can buy. It's about what you can walk away from: bad deals, wrong clients, models that no longer serve.

Independence is having genuine options in daily decisions:

- Turning down profitable work that doesn't align
- Taking real vacation without checking email
- Investing in five-year improvements rather than quarterly fixes
- Choosing clients based on fit rather than revenue
- Supporting causes without worrying about cost

During acquisition negotiations, personal wealth provides what money can't directly buy: time to wait for the right opportunity. When buyers try last-minute price reductions—a common tactic against desperate sellers—you can walk away. Better buyers with better terms often follow.

# Full Circle

We started with a gap: business owners managing million-dollar operations while personal wealth sat neglected. Optimizing everything in the company while accepting whatever someone else set up for personal finances.

Now, that same strategic thinking coordinates your complete financial picture. The quarterly rhythm runs automatically. Your owner advantages work for you, not against you. Every business season becomes navigable because your wealth building doesn't depend on any single quarter's performance.

You've built something more valuable than assets—a system where business success and personal wealth strengthen each other. Where your best business decisions aren't driven by personal pressure. Where family security doesn't depend on quarterly performance.

The business you built proves you can build wealth. The wealth you're building proves the business works without consuming you. Each makes the other more valuable.

That's the ultimate Owner's Dividend—not just financial security, but the freedom to lead and live on your own terms.

## KEY TAKEAWAY

When you systematically turn business success into personal wealth, you don't just build assets—you become the leader your business always needed, collecting dividends that extend far beyond financial returns.

| Owner's Checklist | | |
|---|---|---|
| Metric to watch | Conversation to schedule | Action within 30 days |
| Can you turn down profitable work that doesn't fit your strategy? | With key stakeholders: "What could we walk away from now that we couldn't before?" | Exercise one new option your wealth has created—say no to something you would have said yes to before |

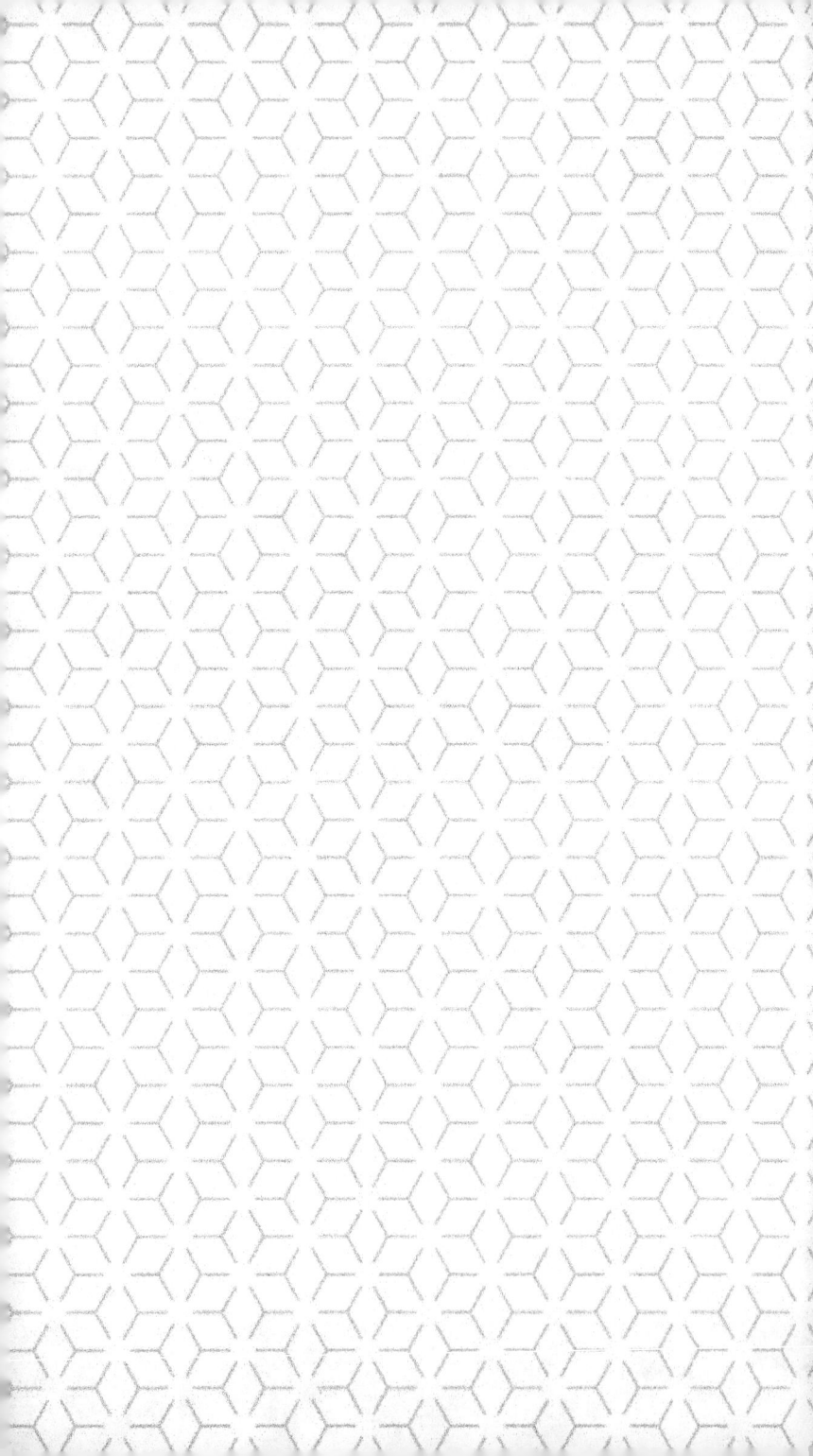

# CONCLUSION

Throughout my career working with business owners, I've observed the same pattern enough times to know it's not coincidence.

The owners who successfully build wealth alongside their businesses aren't necessarily smarter or more disciplined than those who don't. They simply encountered the right framework at the right time. Someone showed them that the challenges they were experiencing—the variable cash flow, the tax complexity, the concentration risk—weren't unique to them. These challenges are inherent to business ownership itself. And what's inherent to the system can be systematically addressed.

Growing up in my family's manufacturing business gave me my deep respect for entrepreneurs. I watched my parents build something from nothing, create jobs, serve customers, and navigate every challenge with creativity and grit. That experience taught me what business ownership requires—the responsibility, the resourcefulness, the relentless drive forward. It also showed me what was missing from the conversation: how to systematically turn that business success into personal financial security.

Later, working with owners who'd successfully sold their businesses, I saw what became possible when someone built wealth methodically during operations, not hopefully after exit. The difference wasn't about talent or luck. It was having a system.

The gap between business success and personal wealth isn't about working harder or earning more. It's about knowing the system exists and implementing it.

That's why I wrote this book—because business owners deserve planning designed for how they actually operate. You've already done the hardest part. The rest is just applying what you know to what you've been missing.

# APPENDIX

## Business-Owner Financial Health Assessment

This five-minute self-assessment gauges how your personal finances align with your business. Use it to see where you stand today. There are no wrong answers.

**Why These Four Areas:** They represent the foundation of owner wealth building—diversification, liquidity, consistency, and coordination.

**Wealth Diversification** — *lower concentration risk*

1. What portion of your total wealth is held outside your business?

   ☐ Less than 10%
   ☐ 10-20%
   ☐ 20-30%
   ☐ More than 30%

   *Keeping more than 70-80% of total wealth in any single asset—including your company—can increase concentration risk.*

**Financial Runway** — *cushion for volatility*

2. If business income stopped today, how many months could personal savings cover living expenses?

   ☐ Less than 3 months
   ☐ 3-6 months
   ☐ 6-12 months
   ☐ More than 12 months

   *Many owners target six to twelve months of personal reserves; more may be appropriate in highly cyclical industries.*

**Systematic Wealth Building** — *freedom outside the firm*

3. Are you consistently building wealth outside your business?

   ☐ Not yet
   ☐ Irregularly when cash allows
   ☐ Monthly or quarterly
   ☐ Systematically with professional guidance

   *Regular contributions—however small—can compound meaningfully over time.*

**Professional Coordination** — *turn silos into synergy*

4.  How coordinated is your planning across
    business and personal finances?

    ☐ Handled separately
    ☐ Some CPA check-ins
    ☐ Regular coordination
    ☐ Fully integrated team

    *Coordinated planning can improve tax efficiency and
    risk management.*

**Retirement Clarity** — *knowing your target*

5.  Do you know your actual "enough" number
    for retirement?

    ☐ No idea
    ☐ Rough guess
    ☐ Calculated estimate
    ☐ Detailed plan with timeline

    *Without a target, you can't know if you're on track or how
    hard the business needs to work.*

**Your Score Scoring:**

| | |
|---|---|
| First option | = 1 point |
| Second option | = 2 |
| Third option | = 3 |
| Fourth option | = 4 |
| **Total:** | _____ **out of 20** |

**Important:** *Any individual category scoring 1 requires
immediate attention regardless of total score.*

| Range | Meaning |
|-------|---------|
| **16-20** | Strong foundation |
| **13-15** | Good progress |
| **8-12** | Significant opportunities |
| **Below 8** | Immediate attention needed |

### Interpret Your Result

- Strong foundation (16-20): Solid footing. Periodic review recommended.
- Good progress (13-15): Generally on track. Address lower-scoring domains next.
- Significant opportunities (8-12): Elevated concentration risk. Consider increasing liquidity and external diversification.
- Immediate attention (<8): High risk. Consider building personal reserves and consulting qualified advisors.

## Three Reflection Questions

1. What is this business actually building for you?
2. If you stepped away tomorrow, what would you have left?
3. Would your family know what to do, or be left guessing?

# 12-MONTH OWNER'S DIVIDEND IMPLEMENTATION ROAD MAP

S tart this road map any time of year. Each quarter builds on the previous, moving you from financial dependence to strategic control.

---

## Quarter 1:
## Foundation Building (Months 1-3) Goal

*Establish baseline metrics and begin systematic wealth building*

### Key Actions

- Calculate baseline diversification:
  **Outside-business assets ÷ total net worth**
- Measure personal liquidity runway:
  **Cash ÷ annual household spending**

- Open dedicated personal investment account (separate from business)
- Make your first transfer—even just $1,000—to prove the business can pay you
- Draft one-page personal balance sheet (assets and debts outside the company)
- Schedule spouse/partner conversation about current numbers and goals
- Start tracking your "boring index" (months you don't tinker with investments)

### Success Marker

First transfer completed, baseline metrics calculated, spouse aligned on direction.

---

## Quarter 2:
## Systems Building (Months 4-6) Goal

### Create automatic systems and establish professional coordination

### Key Actions

- Set up automatic monthly transfers (start with 5% of average monthly profit)
- Review personal cash efficiency: Keep 6-month runway, invest the rest
- Consider how your plan would handle a 30-50% revenue drop
- Schedule joint CPA + advisor meeting to coordinate tax strategies
- Begin connecting business cycles to personal transfers

- Increase transfer amount once if system is working smoothly

## *Success Marker*

Automated transfers running for 2+ months, professional team talking to each other, excess cash working harder.

---

## Quarter 3:
## Business Integration (Months 7-9) Goal

*Align wealth building with business cycles and address owner-specific gaps*

## *Key Actions:*

- Map your 12-month cash-flow patterns (mark surge and slow months)
- Adjust transfer amounts to match business seasonality
- Address your biggest owner gap from chapter 7 (e.g., liquidity, tax timing, exit planning)
- Test raising transfers during a strong month
- Document one operational improvement you made to sustain transfers
- Calculate months of personal runway gained since Quarter 1

## *Success Marker*

Wealth building flows with business cycles, transfers continue through ups and downs, business operations improving to support systematic payments.

## Quarter 4:
## Strategic Control (Months 10-12) Goal:

*Achieve systematic wealth building
and test true independence*

### Key Actions

- Calculate "boring index"
  **Months with zero investment tweaks ÷ 12 (target: 9+)**

- Confirm your phase: Foundation, Systems, or Strategic Confidence

- Schedule quarterly Wealth Review one week after business QBR

- Delegate one business decision you previously hoarded

- Plan independence test
  **Two-week vacation without checking business accounts**

- List three financial decisions you made without checking business cash first

### Success Marker

You're measuring success by what you can walk away from, not just what you can buy.

# Ongoing:
## Systematic Wealth Building Goal:

*Maintain momentum and measure
true independence*

### Monthly Rhythm

- Automatic transfers execute (no decisions required)
- Track business decisions made from financial pressure (target: zero)
- Maintain separation between business performance and personal security

### Quarterly Discipline

- Update personal balance sheet
- Compare progress to annual milestones
- Adjust transfer amounts based on business cycles
- Review, then ignore until next quarter

### 12-Month Success Indicators

You know the system is working when:

- Personal wealth grows regardless of quarterly business performance
- You make business decisions based on strategy, not cash flow pressure
- Market volatility doesn't affect your sleep
- You can evaluate opportunities without personal financial anxiety
- Your "boring index" consistently exceeds 75%

- Your business runs better because systematic transfers forced operational improvements

### The Ultimate Test

Can you take a two-week vacation without checking business accounts, knowing both your company and personal wealth will continue building value without your daily involvement?

When the answer is yes, you've successfully implemented the Owner's Dividend system.

# A Note on Implementation

This road map covers the foundation. Working with an advisor who specializes in business owners unlocks the advanced strategies—retirement plan design, entity optimization, tax coordination across business and personal—that transform good results into exceptional ones.

# What's Next?

Completing this 12-month road map means you've successfully built your foundation (Phase 1 of 4). The journey continues with Systems + Psychology (Years 2-3), Strategic Confidence (Years 3-5+), and ultimately Full Independence (Year 5+) when your business becomes most valuable precisely when you need it least.

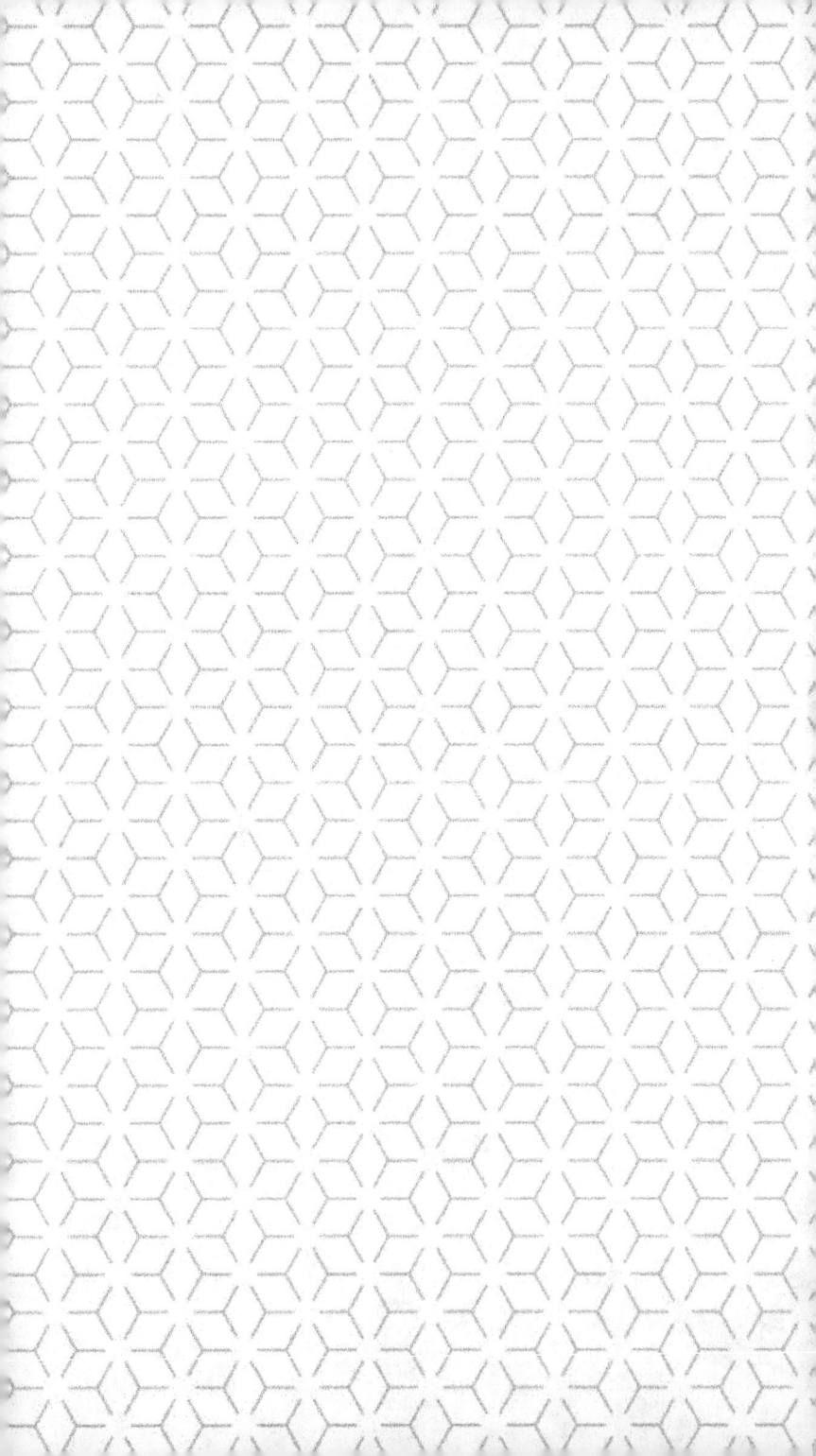

# ABOUT THE AUTHOR

**Caroline McInerney** helps business owners build personal wealth as systematically as they built their companies.

Growing up in her family's manufacturing business, Caroline learned firsthand that business success and personal wealth require different but complementary strategies. This understanding shaped her path through both institutional and independent advisory firms before founding HWM Wealth, where she now works with owners throughout their journey—from early-stage entrepreneurs to families who have successfully exited.

With an MBA from Vanderbilt University, Caroline is a CERTIFIED FINANCIAL PLANNER® professional (CFP®) and a Certified Business Exit Consultant (CBEC®). She creates comprehensive wealth strategies that align with how business owners operate.

Based in Atlanta, Caroline works with business owners nationwide who are ready to turn their business success into lasting personal wealth.